PALMISTRY

apprentice to pro in 24 hours

Johnny Fincham

D0753899

Winchester, UK
Washington, USA)

First published by O Books, 2007
Reprinted 2008
O Books is an imprint of John Hunt Publishing Ltd.,
The Bothy, Deershot Lodge, Park Lane, Ropley, Hants, SO24 0BE, UK
office1@o-books.net
www.o-books.net

Distribution in:

UK and Europe
Orca Book Services
orders@orcabookservices.co.uk
Tel: 01202 665432 Fax: 01202 666219 Int. code (44)

USA and Canada
NBN
custserv@nbnbooks.com
Tel: 1 800 462 6420 Fax: 1 800 338 4550

Australia and New Zealand
Brumby Books
sales@brumbybooks.com.au
Tel: 61 3 9761 5535 Fax: 61 3 9761 7095

Far East (offices in Singapore, Thailand, Hong Kong, Taiwan)
Pansing Distribution Pte Ltd
kemal@pansing.com
Tel: 65 6319 9939 Fax: 65 6462 5761

South Africa
Alternative Books
altbook@peterhyde.co.za
Tel: 021 447 5300 Fax: 021 447 1430

Text copyright Johnny Fincham 2007

Design: Stuart Davies
Cover: Deluxe Design

ISBN-13: 978 1 84694 047 7

A CIP catalogue record for this book is available from the British Library.

Printed in the US by Maple Vail

PALMISTRY

apprentice to pro in 24 hours

Johnny Fincham

BOOKS

Winchester, UK
Washington, USA

ACKNOWLEDGEMENTS

This book is dedicated to my many students and clients over the years who have taught me so much. Also thanks to Christopher Jones and to lovely Laura Abbro for fastidious editing.

CONTENTS

INTRODUCTION

Despite being as old as civilization itself, palmistry has been obscured by more myths, mumbo-jumbo and superstition than almost any other subject on earth.

The legacy of chiromancy (which means to predict the future from markings on the palm or from any natural signs), has obscured the astonishing potential of palmistry as a tool for self-development. The idea that one's fate is fixed is a legacy of a medieval life-view. One which undermines an individual's sense of responsibility and diminishes the power they have over their lives.

Modern palmistry is often known as 'chirology', which is from the Greek for 'hand study'. Chirology is associated with a more enlightened approach to the art, performing in-depth, non-predictive palm analysis for self-understanding. This perspective has attained the 'upper hand' amongst most of today's palmists and is winning the respect of cynics and scientists alike. Over four thousand research papers have been published on aspects of the palm, finding strong correlations between hand features and psychological disposition, genetic illnesses, sexual attractiveness and even the likelihood of success in sports – all of which correlates with the principles of palmistry.

As an art, palmistry has been studied by the greatest minds in history, including Aristotle, Plato, Julius Speer and Karl Jung. All the great civilizations have included palmistry in their culture, including the ancient Chinese, Hebrews, Egyptians, Hindus, Tibetans and Babylonians. The pedigree of this discipline then, is impeccable.

In the past twenty years, a huge number of people have

become fascinated by the insightful arts, like tarot, astrology and numerology. Through an understanding of these ancient skills they've found a deeper meaning and new perspectives on life.

The number of those that practice palmistry however (arguably the most powerful of the 'insightful arts') is relatively few. The reason for this is because the subject has traditionally been difficult to master. A major hurdle is that most instructional books and courses are either overly simplistic or they present the student with a bewildering array of mounts, markings and line patterns to commit to memory. Added to this is an antiquated language and ideas that have little relevance today. Lines of fate and rings of Saturn, mystic crosses and stars of fortune owe more to sorcery than common sense. The lines supposedly indicating the sex and number of children a person will have, for instance, are downright silly. Most sinister marks and fated signs in many modern palmistry books have changed little since medieval times.

This book will change all that. Here you'll acquire a set of straightforward principles enabling you to develop a palmistry technique that's devastatingly powerful, yet simple to practice. You'll learn a new language of the hand, free of references to fate, stars and fortune; a palmistry lexicon that accurately expresses the quality of each palm feature. If other books have left you confused, don't worry, this one won't. Absolutely anyone can learn to be a palmist, with no prior knowledge whatsoever.

Let's get a few facts straight. The lines of the palm aren't fixed. They change over time (and in very little time the case of minor lines). It goes without saying then, that if you're going make predictions based on the palm's lines, you're not going to get accurate results. No one can tell you your future by looking at your hand. No crocks of gold or tall dark strangers are marked there.

It's also impossible to tell the age at which you'll die; the cities you'll visit and the color of your grandmother's eyes. All of which, I assure you, are questions you'll be expected to answer once it becomes known you're a palmist.

It may certainly be possible to intuit these things, and there's no doubt that looking into people's souls through the window of the hands will bring out your latent intuitive facilities. Right from the start, however, with no help from psychic sources, you can quickly acquire the skill to amaze, the insight to bring change, the wisdom to enlighten and empower.

'A man's character is his fate' said Heraclitus (in 500 BC) and indeed, the person we are creates the future we make for ourselves. It is not, however, the shackles of destiny we palmists seek to bind folk with, but the freedom to create a new future through positive change that we offer through the light of our guidance.

If you believe in a fixed fate and that free will is a myth, then this book will disappoint you. But if you would plumb the depths of the human soul; if you would pinpoint deep psychological quirks and quandaries and liberate people from them; if you would offer folk the chance to start again with a new understanding of their potentials; if you would practice a modern form of magic with a new dimension on the meaning of life and a study that will fascinate you forever – then you have chosen well.

How to get the most from this book

This book has been written as a result of twenty years of teaching palmistry, refining continually what works and what doesn't. Only if a sign on the palm works a thousand times over on a thousand

examples has it made it into this book. All negative, confusing and downright inaccurate traditional palmistry interpretations have been ditched. All traditional palmistry names for markings and features have been replaced with new and descriptive labels that make their meaning clear (though the traditional labels are provided for reference). The Jupiter finger for instance (which is about self-reflection) is renamed the mirror digit.

Everything here works. You have only to put the knowledge into practice. Many of my students have gone on to work as professional palmists. Whether or not this is your ambition you will find the tools here to astonish yourself and anyone you read for. Before we begin, though, let's start with the five golden palmistry rules.

The rules

The first rule: **proceed slowly**. Try to see a palm reading as an *investigation*. You're looking for subtle markings and lineal formations that simply can't be grasped in a quick glance. You need to approach the palm like a detective, investigating the scene-of-crime evidence, seeing in the tiniest detail, a fingerprint, a fork in a line, a pattern in the skin, a wealth of information. So don't rush.

The second rule: **ignore anything average**. This will save you an enormous amount of time. No one wants to know how average and normal they are. Individuality reveals itself in markings that are individual. Each one of us is unique and this is revealed in some unusual marking on the palm. No two hands are the same (even those of identical twins). You're always looking for something that defines a person. If you see, say, an ulnar loop print on the index finger (as you will see, this is an extremely common marking) this is of no consequence.

The third rule: **do your homework**. Practice constantly. Every point you learn will be followed by an example. Every chapter will be followed by practice points. If you complete these before moving on, you'll learn much more quickly.

Fourth rule: **give palm readings only when you feel ready**. By all means test out the points you learn on friends and relatives. Use them to see examples of hand features you're looking for. The danger is that people have a habit of expecting you to sort their life problems out for them when you look at their palms. Don't let yourself come under this kind of pressure too early. You'll soon be able to offer incredibly useful advice and life-changing insights. However, in the beginning, just ask people questions to confirm your judgments: 'would you describe yourself as very sensitive?'

for instance, is a good approach.

Fifth rule: **read the whole palm**. No one point should be taken on its own as a value judgment. The obsessive feelings you see in the Line of Emotion may well be balanced by a great deal of self-disciple in a thumb that's particularly stiff, for example. A person is the sum of many contradictory and complementary aspects, so balance your observations and put them together to form a complete picture.

Now we've established the ground rules, we're almost ready to go, but hold on a minute! Remember rules one and three: *don't rush* and *do your homework*. In this book we'll easily cover all you need to know through twenty-four, one-hour chapters. However, I strongly recommend you devote yourself to covering no more than one chapter in a single day, making sure you complete the assignments that follow. Most of us gain little by studying for more than an hour at a time anyway. Give yourself the rest of each day to practice and consolidate what you've learned. This way, you can become a serious palm reader within a month. Let's go!

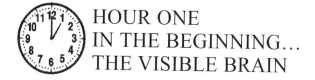

HOUR ONE
IN THE BEGINNING...
THE VISIBLE BRAIN

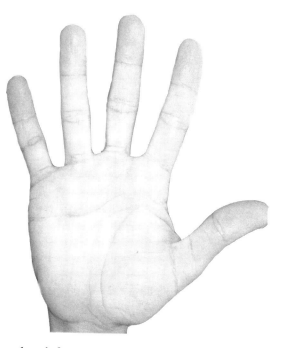

Look at your hand for a moment. Stretch back the fingers and thumb so the lines show up.

Intriguing isn't it? The network of lines marked there has fascinated man since history began. A colossal number of motor and neuron connections in the brain are devoted to the hand, out of all proportion to their physical dimensions. The portion of the brain devoted to the hands and fingers is fourteen times larger than that assigned to the face, for instance. If the hands were represented in equal ratio to the other parts of the body in the human brain they'd need to be the size of beach umbrellas!

No wonder the palms are often called the 'visible brain'.

The human body shown in proportion to each area's share of the cerebral cortex

Palm printing

In modern practice, many readers work from a print rather than the palm itself, because more detail is revealed on a print than can be seen on the bare palm. You'll probably find yourself working from both flesh-and-blood palm and print. It's advisable to take prints whenever possible, because with a print, you can watch and record the changes in the lines over time. Another benefit is that you can study someone's palm print in private, without feeling pressured to read for them. You'll find print-taking instructions at the back of this book in Appendix 1.

Right or left?

Which hand should you read – the right or the left? Many traditional palmistry books will tell you that the future is marked in the right hand (assuming a person is right handed) while the past is marked in the left.

It's actually different and more subtle than that. The active hand (as the right hand is called on a right-hander) is the expression of the outward personality. Here you'll find the developed, conscious, real-world expression of who and what you are. Usually the active hand has clearer and stronger lines marked on it. This is because we tend to be more focused and concentrated in our active, day-to-day experience than we are in our more reflective personality.

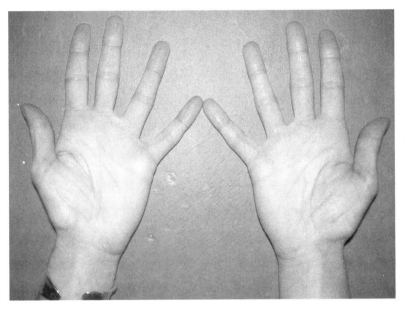

The passive hand is the subconscious, reflective, private self. The hurts and joys from childhood and the influences of your parents are buried here. The qualities of our passive hands are often hidden; they only come out in our personal experiences. Only a partner, family member or intimate friend would know a person as they are reflected in their passive hand.

You should give more attention to the active hand on someone over 21 years of age and more to the passive hand if younger than this. But always read *both* hands and compare them constantly. The greater the difference between the two hands the more the person is changing and developing. Both hands change over time.

If your client is ambidextrous, or if you're not sure which is the active hand, compare the stiffness of the thumbs. Hold each thumb and pull it back away from the index finger toward the wrist. The hand with the *stiffest* thumb is the active hand.

Ignore the shape, discount the mounts

For centuries, palmists have attempted to define personality by the shape of a person's palms. They allocated a particular character type to a particular palm formation. People were given labels like the philosophic, the primitive, the psychic and the practical type, depending on whether they had square, narrow, long or short palms.

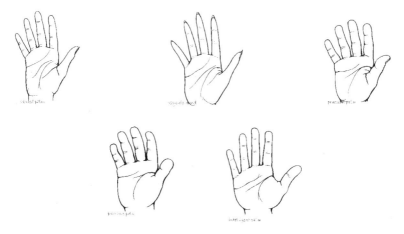

Classic palm shapes

Unfortunately, this simplistic practice does not give accurate results. People are complicated and the matching of palm shape to a personality just doesn't work except in the crudest terms and in very specific circumstances. The only correspondence you'll notice about hand shape is that it's related to body type. The finger sections (known as phalanges) correspond to the length of the limbs. You'll find people with broad, heavy palms and short fingers will have stocky bodies and short limbs. Those with long fingers and narrower, flatter palms will tend to be more willowy with longer limbs.

As a tool for personality divination we can safely ignore the palm shape.

The palm mounts we shall also ignore. Historically, palmists have given great emphasis to the mounts and they still feature strongly in most palmistry books.

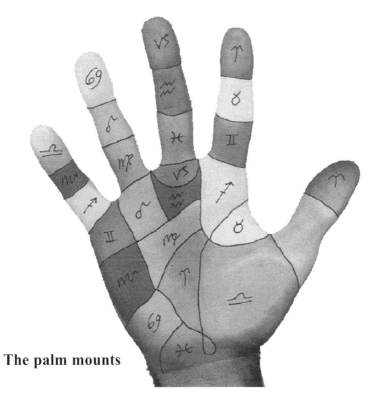

The palm mounts

The mounts are a legacy of a time when astrological principles were considered the major influence on human experience. The mounts are ruled by various planets and were used as a measure of their effects on the individual personality. However, they have been proven to be of no consequence and we shall not waste our time on them.

Squeeze me, please me!

OK! Enough theory. It's time to get down to business of palmistry proper. Here we'll examine the consistency of the flesh at the base of the palm near the thumb. From this we can find out a huge amount about a person's basic energy and physical resources.

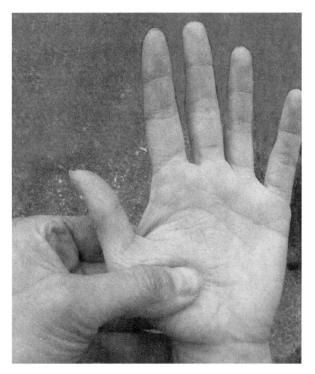

Squeezing the thumb ball - this one is soft and easily crushed

Take the hand of the person you're reading for in your own. Press your thumb into the flesh around their thumb ball while gripping the back of the palm with your fingers.

Beneath the semi-circular fleshy padding around the thumb's base is the hand's major artery which splits here into various smaller blood vessels. The protective padding here - its size, warmth and firmness - is a good indicator of a person's general muscle development, blood circulation, zest for life and physical resources.

Full but flabby

If the flesh forms a full and high mound, but it's flabby, so the pad is easily crushed, there's acute sensuality but poor muscular development. This is particularly true if the palm skin is also moist. People with such qualities are pleasure-seekers who love food, drink and the pleasures of the flesh. They can find it difficult to diet and are inclined to make hard work of exercise. The key here is to encourage them to find a form of exercise they enjoy, i.e. swimming or dancing.

Full and firm

If the flesh here is full, firm, warm and springy, it shows a passionate, lusty vitality, abundant energy and human warmth.

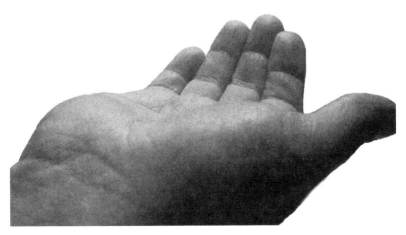

A full, firm thumb ball

Firm, full and hard

When the pad is full but rock hard (almost as if made of wood) the person has enormous physical toughness. They're extremely hardy, emotively repressive and rather rigid psychologically. Good advice to give is for them to have regular massage treatments. This will release tight muscles physically and open them out emotionally.

Flat and cold

If the fleshy pad is flat and cold, there is a consequent lassitude, emotional coolness and lack of vital energy, but often a stubborn resilience.

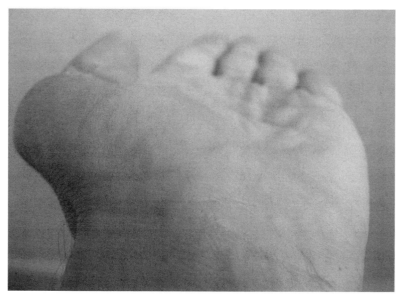

A flat thumb ball

Such people should be advised to do aerobic exercise, which will increase circulation and lift energy levels.

The unremarkable average

If the pad is half-raised and fairly firm, this is a general average. Maintaining our golden rule of ignoring anything average, we'll dismiss this sign of a fair but unremarkable quality of vital energy.

Secret palmist assignment

While you're learning palmistry, try to keep it a secret from the world at large until you've gained plenty of experience. Once people know you're a palmist, you may get trampled in the rush as everyone thrusts their palm in your face! This can be intimidating; you need to gain confidence quietly while remaining incognito. Use only trusted friends and relatives as your initial 'guinea pigs'.

Get into the habit of being a secret palm-watcher. Examine people's hands from a distance - see if you can see a relationship between the length of the fingers and the length of someone's limbs. Look at the size of the thumb ball on people's hands. If you shake someone's hand, try to feel this area. Observe how those with full, firm thumb balls are vital, energetic people and those with a flat mount the reverse.

Brain bashing quiz
Time given: ten minutes

1. Are the palms represented in equal proportion to the rest of the body in the cerebral cortex?
2. What does the word 'chirology' mean?
3 Does the passive hand show the person you were in a

previous lifetime?

4 How would you check for the active hand on an ambidextrous person?

5 What can you tell from the hand shape? Be careful with this one!

6 What can be measured by the palm mounts? Think before you answer!

7 What does it mean to have a full, but soft, easily-crushed thumb ball? Would an athlete display this feature?

8 What about a full, firm thumb ball? This one is so easy!

9 What advice might you give someone with a rock hard thumb ball?

Answers are on the next page.

HOUR TWO
THE SKIN'S THE THING

Touch me Feel me!

Now to the skin texture. This is a major point of reference for the palmist. The skin on the inside of the palm is covered with a multitude of fine ridges, barely visible to the naked eye. Within the ridges are embedded a host of various types of nerve sensors for heat, moisture, temperature, pain and so on. The finer the skin, the higher number of skin ridges present and the greater the number of nerve endings. The palm skin tells you about the kind of environment a person naturally responds to, the level of refinement of their central nervous system and their overall receptivity to stimuli.

Naturally, someone with fine, delicate palm skin may develop calluses after a prolonged spell of gardening or physical labor. However, the skin will soon return to its normal condition once this activity stops. The skin quality indicates our preferred environment and we don't tend to stray out of it for long.

Answers

1. The palms neurone and motor nerve supply in the human cortex is out of all proportion to their physical size. Proportionate to the rest of the body, they'd need to be the size of beach umbrellas.
2. 'Chirology' is derived from the Greek for 'hand study'.
3. No. The passive hand is the deeper, subconscious, private personality.
4. The active hand is found by checking the stiffness of the thumbs. The stiffest thumb is on the active hand.
5. The hand shape is of no use for personality divination. However, it shows a relationship between digit length and limb length.
6. Measuring the palm mounts is of no use whatever.
7. An athlete would be unlikely to display an easily crushed thumb ball. It's the sign of a sensual, pleasure loving person.
8. A full, firm thumb ball is the sign of a vital, energetic person.
9. Someone with a rock hard thumb ball needs to have a regular massage.

The skin ridges

The thicker the skin, the fewer messages get though and the less one picks up from one's surroundings. The finer and more delicate the skin on the inside of the palm, the more one is receptive to subtle stimuli from the atmosphere. No matter what other indicators there are on the palm about the sensitivity of an individual, the skin is the primary and constant indicator about how responsive a person is.

Clammy skin

Damp skin denotes heightened sensitivity, anxiety and over-wrought emotions. This may be only temporary, perhaps a person is nervous of having their palm read, or they may be worked up about something. When the skin is permanently moist, it shows a person strongly ruled by their emotions. This isn't necessarily a sign of being sensitive, however.

Skin quality

To judge the skin quality, stroke the index fingertip of your active

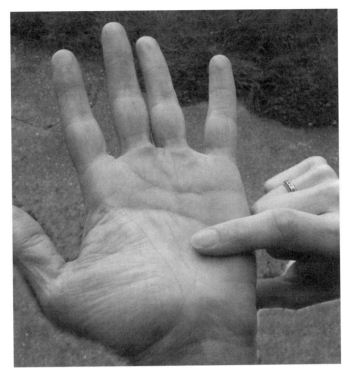

checking the skin type

hand (this is the most sensitive fingertip) over the central area of the palm.

The palm skin quality is split into four descriptive categories: silk, paper, grainy and coarse.

At this point, it's worth bearing in mind that everything in the palm has both positive and negative aspects. Every line, marking and feature can be an asset or a hindrance depending on how well the bearer understands themselves. Your job as a palmist is to give them as much information as possible, pointing out the pitfalls and advantages of every feature you see. Be kind, be positive, but be truthful.

Silk skin

If the skin feels fragile, silky smooth, delicate and thin, you have an example of the finest skin type - *silk* skin. It really does feel like you're brushing your fingertip over a piece of silk, the skin ridges are so fine as to be barely detectable. There's an immediate impression of delicacy with such skin.

Silk skin gives the greatest degree of sensitivity, and is found on about one fifth of the population. It's more common on women's hands than men's.

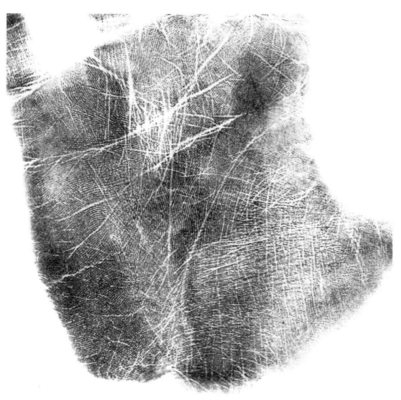

Print of a silk-skinned palm – the skin ridges are almost too fine to be seen

People with silk skin are very receptive, often psychic and intensely aware. They tune in to 'vibes' and atmospheres, they can detect the faintest trace of tannin in the wine, they can feel the aftershock of a past argument in the room they've just entered. Usually they're pale-skinned as they like to avoid the sun.

Silk-skinned people are subtle, avoiding the loud and obvious. They tend to be fastidious in dress and personal hygiene, finding it stressful to be grubby or to be in a room that's untidy. They are prone to skin problems, digestive and nervous disorders, allergies and phobias. They aren't able to tolerate alcohol, a couple of cocktails and a beer after work would knock a silk-skinned soul flat.

You may find the thumb ball with this type of skin is easily crushed (signifying lack of vigor). This skin pattern gives a need to be in peaceful and harmonious situations. It's found on alternative therapists, infant teachers, care workers, healers, some artists, spiritual aspirants and religious professionals.

It's amazing how commonly you find someone with silk skin struggling along in an inappropriate environment. They're never happy in stressful jobs in aggressive surroundings, like double glazing sales or debt collection. Whenever you find someone with silk skin, it's essential that the person is advised to avoid toxins and harsh environments, and to value their sensitivity.

Paper skin

When the skin feels fine and dry and is often slightly yellowish in color, it is *paper* skin. The skin ridges are just perceptible under your fingertip.

This skin ridge density is very common, found on around half of hands in the modern city environment. It's found in equal proportion on men's and woman's hands.

This pattern, though definitely on the sensitive side, isn't fine enough for intuitive perceptions. People with paper skin respond to visual, verbal and information-based stimuli. They like to be in an environment where there's an exchange of *ideas*.

Communication is important, people with this palm skin have a flair for and are responsive to sound and images, words and pictures. The passions are kept under wraps, on first meeting they're likely to appear a little 'cool'.

Usually this skin type is accompanied by a thumb ball that's a little on the flat side (signifying emotional coolness).

Paper skin type is very common. The sort of surroundings you can expect a person with paper skin to be in is anywhere surrounded by words, images, paper, phones and computers – a lawyer, teacher, salesperson, web designer, office worker, student, writer, and all the realm of the media.

Grainy skin

The next level in our skin gradient is *grainy* skin. This is where the skin ridges are clearly visible and easily felt. The skin feels just slightly rough, with well-defined lines.

This skin pattern is more common on men's hands than women's and shows a person who isn't particularly sensitive. This skin type indicates a need for activity and stimulus. This is someone with quick responses, who's easily bored and who likes to keep active. They have good reflexes and a sense of timing and potentially are good at sports. Usually people with this skin type work hard and play hard and get stuck into life. The thumb ball is usually well developed with this skin (signifying abundant zest).

These characters need to be active and are not really of sufficient sensitivity to enjoy passive activities, i.e. tone chanting/meditation, for very long. They are uncomfortable with gushing displays of emotion. Relaxation is often difficult; usually they prefer to let off steam in some kind of active leisure activity, like skiing. Grainy-skinned people always have a busy day ahead of them. You'll find them in business and pressured, incentive-driven working environments. They should be guided to get themselves in active, stimulating surroundings and into sports and hobbies that give life a buzz.

Coarse skin

'Coarse skin' is easy to measure. The skin is thick, hard and rough to the touch – almost abrasive.

Here is someone who responds to the physical world. They need to be in the great outdoors; anyone with coarse skin would hate to be stuck indoors for very long. This level of skin induces a rapport with nature, and the world of material things. They're likely to posses manual skills, be very hardy and almost indifferent to pain and temperature.

The broad furrow-like skin ridges make the person coarse and thick skinned. They may not notice they've knocked the tip off their finger laying bricks or that they offended someone by not wearing the correct tie at the works party. Such folk are impervious to hardship. Usually the thumb ball is extremely flat and hard. There are very few palm lines and this pattern is found almost exclusively on men.

Coarse skin is common on farmers, fishermen, builders, manual workers, carpenters, potters, mechanics and window

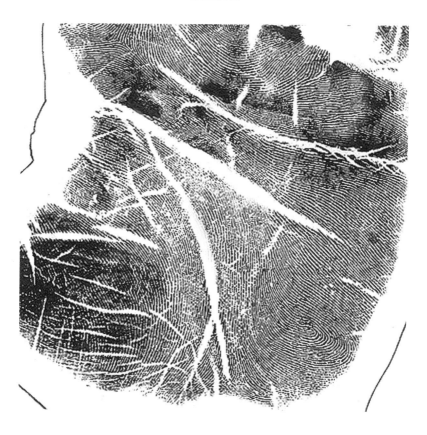

Print of a coarse-skinned palm – the skin ridges are easily visible

cleaners. They tend to loathe over-formal situations, and are repressive with their emotions. It's important that coarse-skinned people are encouraged to talk about themselves.

Secret palmist assignment

You need to experience an example of each skin type so you can identify it quickly.

Start with the palms of your friends and relatives. You'll soon find the more sensitive and receptive a person is, the finer their palm skin tends to be. Shake hands with as many people as possible. Try to make connections between their palm skin and their personality type. You'll find course skin on the outdoor worker, grainy skin on the active type, paper skin on the computer programmer and silk skin on the psychic healer.

Brain bashing quiz
Time given: ten minutes

1. What does the skin texture on the inside of the palm tell you about a person?
2. Does coarse skin make a person sensitive to the atmosphere around them?
3. Are there more nerve sensors embedded in grainy skin than silk skin?
4. Would a silk-skinned person make a good night-club bouncer?
5. Would a paper-skinned person make good outdoor worker?
6. What skin type would be most at home in an office?
7. What skin type would a sports person be likely to have?
8. Which skin type is the most indifferent to pain?
9. Which skin type is the most sensitive to toxins?

Answers are on the next page.

HOUR THREE
THUMBS UP - THE RUDDER OF PERSONALITY

The rule of thumb

The thumbs are what make humans unique among mammals. It's the single development that enabled mankind to dominate his environment (apes have only tiny, underdeveloped thumbs). The thumb provides opposition to the fingers and our ability to form a gripping motion. This is the evolutionary key that allowed man to make tools and shape the world around him.

The thumb is a measure of your 'grip' on life. The bigger and stiffer the thumb, the greater your capacity to get a grip of yourself and exert self-control. A weaker thumbed person is more self-indulgent and more likely to let opportunities slip from their grasp.

Think of the thumb as the rudder of the personality. It holds you to the course you've set yourself. A big stiff thumb is like a large fixed rudder that will steer a person to any particular goal or ambition, be it climbing a mountain, sticking to a diet or learning French. A small, bendy thumb will be strongly affected by the

Answers
1. The skin quality on the inside of the palm tells a palmist about the density of the skin ridges and therefore about a person's responsiveness to their environment and the sensitivity of their central nervous system.
2. No. Coarse skin is the least sensitive.
3. No. Silk skin has the highest number of nerve sensors.
4. No. A silk-skinned person is too sensitive for this work.
5. No. A paper-skinned person is best suited to a visual, verbal and information based environment.
6. Paper-skinned people make the best office workers.
7. Grainy-skinned people have quick reflexes and make the best sportspeople.
8. Coarse-skinned people are the most indifferent to pain.
9. Silk-skinned people are the most sensitive to toxins.

currents, winds and tides of life and more easily drawn off-course by the influence of others.

When you study the thumb you're studying an individual's will power, the control a person has over themselves and over their circumstances.

Reading the thumbs is relatively easy – you only need to check the length and stiffness. Thumbs tend to be similar in terms of length and an extra long or short one will stand out immediately.

Checking thumb length

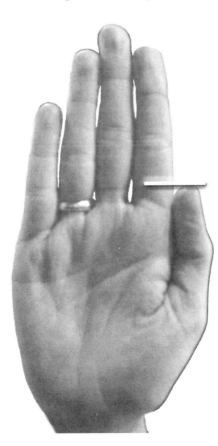

The way to measure the thumb is to lay it alongside the palm keeping the fingers upright.

Measuring the thumb

As long as the thumb reaches *one-quarter to half-way* up the bottom section of the index finger, it's of average length. If it doesn't make it this far (only reaching say, the base crease line of the index finger) it's short; if it reaches more than half-way up the first section, it's long.

A long thumb has abundant reserves of self discipline, persistence, and

Note Bill Gates' long thumb

self mastery. Short thumbs have fewer reserves of persistence and 'stickability' when the going gets tough.

Stiff or floppy?

The next point to check is the thumb's stiffness. In many respects this is the most important thumb quality because it tells you how strongly the person *applies and uses* their will. No matter how long the thumb, if it's loose jointed, an individual won't use what strength of will they posses.

Measuring thumb stiffness

Check the stiffness by placing your own thumb on a person's bottom thumb joint and pull it back (toward the wrist) with your fingers.

A stiff thumb barely moves back when pulled, where a floppy thumb can extend all the way almost to the wrist. One that moves back only an inch or two is average.

A stiff-thumbed person keeps their impulses on a tight rein. They're found on more dominating personalities and those that get what they want through sheer effort. Stiff thumbs can apply themselves rigidly in their approach to endeavors and have little tolerance for those with less self-restraint.

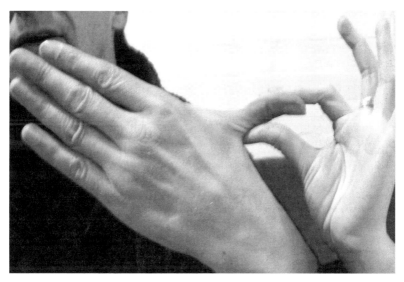

A bendy thumb

A bendy-thumbed person is spontaneous, they'll get distracted and bored easily. They can more easily find themselves 'under the thumb' of a more dominant personality. When on, for instance a strict diet, a floppy thumbed soul will find it much harder to resist the ice-cream.

They're more open, friendly and spontaneous than stiff thumbs though and more adaptable in their approach to goals. They make good 'people' people.

Good advice for someone with a small or floppy thumb is for them to use the help and support of a group to attain their goals. Stiff thumbed individuals should be counseled into loosening up a little and being less hard on themselves.

It's crude, dude

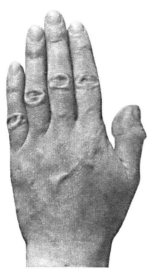

Occasionally you'll come across a thumb that is somewhat stunted, blunt and crude looking, with a tip that's broad and squat. In this case there's a raw primal dimension to the person's energy. They usually possess surprising strength and need a direct physical outlet for their passions.

Secret palmist assignment

Examine the thumbs of ten people you know. See if any of them have a

A broad, blunt thumb

particularly floppy or a stiff thumb. Try to see how their thumb's qualities are reflected in the way they approach personal goals. Take notice of the size of people's thumbs. You'll notice a connection between big thumbs and high achievers.

Brain bashing quiz

Time given: ten minutes

1. Why is the thumb important?

2. Do big-thumbed people have a power complex?

3. What's the difference between floppy and stiff-thumbed personalities?

4. Would a stiff-thumbed person be spontaneous?

5. Would a floppy-thumbed person be a disciplinarian?

6. How long is an average-length thumb – how is it measured?

7. What advice would you give a floppy thumbed person that was about to go on a diet?

8. Are floppy thumbs bad news?

9. What does it mean if the thumb is crude looking, with a blunt, broad tip?

Answers are on the next page.

HOUR FOUR
THE FASCINATING FINGERS

Brain development and finger development

You can get an amazing understanding of a person's psychological motivations from their fingers. The digits show the brain's development of the sense of self (index finger), one's attitude to society (wall finger), the quality of self-expression (ring finger) and communication skills (little finger). A person's balance of these qualities is shown by the balance of these fingers in relation to each-other. As a palmist, you're looking for any digit that's extra-long or short. The relative length of the digits is established as a result of early developmental experiences, and by exposure to various chemical messages being transmitted to the fetus. These primary experiences leave markers in finger length that are very revealing.

Answers

1. The thumbs are the indicator of a person's will-power and self control.
2. No. They have abundant reserves of self discipline, persistence, and self mastery.
3. Floppy thumbed folk don't apply themselves, stiff thumbed people do.
4. It's unlikely. Stiff thumbed folk tend to be quite controlled.
5. It's unlikely. Floppy thumbed folk tend to be lax and easy-going.
6. The thumb is measured by laying it alongside the index digit. As long as it reaches one quarter to one half the way up the lowest phalange of this finger, its of average length.
7. It would be wise to join a group of more highly motivated people.
8. No. Loose thumbed people are open, friendly, spontaneous and adaptable.
9. There's a raw primal dimension to crude thumbed person's energy. They need a direct, physical outlet for their passions.

The long and the short of it

Before we explore the fingers individually, let's check a few points about the digits in general.

First, finger length. Some people have long fingers that almost equal the length of the palm. Some have short fingers that look a little stubby – the digits may be only three-quarters the length of the palm or less.

Bob Dylan – check out those long, long fingers

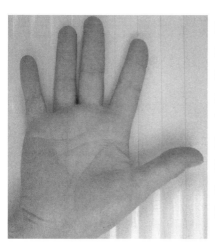

Short fingers

Half the population has medium-length fingers which are of course average and of no consequence.

The longer the fingers, the more a person dwells in abstract, non-physical ideas. A Doctor of philosophy, for instance, would have long fingers

Long-fingered folk think long and hard about everything. They tend to be more sophisticated in their ideas than short-fingered people. They're more critical and introspective. Long-fingered individuals are good with details and tend to specialize in a particular subject.

The opposite pattern, where the fingers are short,

reflects a mentality of 'short' thoughts. This doesn't mean short-fingered people are in any way unintelligent, but mentally they're impatient, holistic and instinctive.

Short-fingered people see the whole picture and have no eye for detail. The shorter the digits, the more a person's thoughts are relative to the physical world. Motor mechanics, for example, have short fingers.

A knotty issue

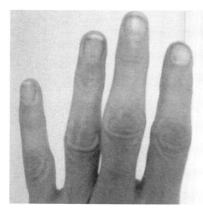

Knotty fingers

On rare occasions, the fingers are knotty, with joints swollen like drumsticks. If this is the case (and as long as the knots aren't caused by arthritis) the effect of the knots is to act as thought processors that 'bounce' ideas around.

Knotty-fingered people are analytical, thorough, argumentative and shrewd.

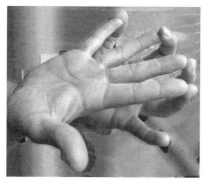

Checking the flexibility of the fingers – these are very stiff

Flexible or rigid minded?

The next thing to check is finger flexibility. You can measure the stiffness of the fingers by drawing them all back at once toward the wrist with your own fingers.

Finger stiffness is a measure

of how 'stiff' the mental processes are. Rigid digits are on rigid-minded people (usually the major joints of the body are stiff as well). If the fingers won't move back more than an inch from the vertical, the person won't adapt to new ideas. They'll be stubborn and lack impulsiveness. Stiff-fingered people have a resilient stubbornness of mind that can push projects through and overcome other's viewpoints by sheer bloody-mindedness.

Flexible fingers (this is where the digits bend back by four inches or more) are mentally impressionable and receptive. They're highly impulsive, with butterfly minds that jump from one subject to another.

Very flexible fingers are always the sign of a flexible mind, and a changeable, spontaneous mind-set.

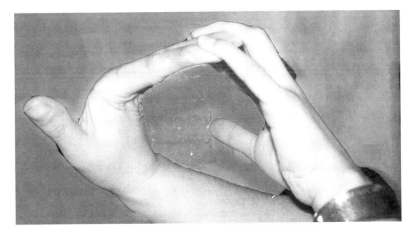

Flexible fingers

Getting the measure of the digits

Here we'll make the crucial check for unusually long or short digits in relationship with each other. When you find one that is extra long or short, its significance will be explained in following

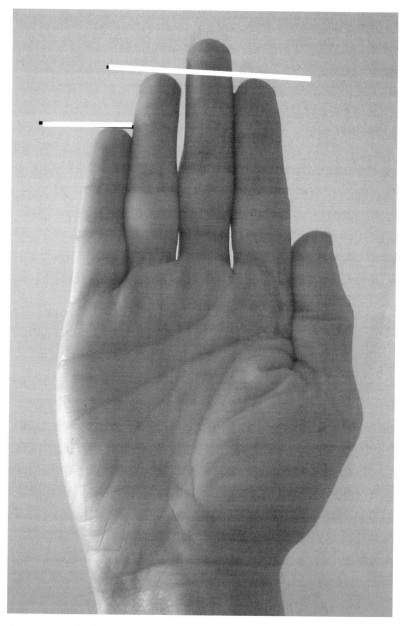

Average relative finger length with fingers standing upright from the palm

chapters.

First make sure the fingers are standing straight up and aren't going off at an angle. If a finger is bent, this makes it shorter, but measure it just the same as if it were straight.

Begin by measuring the difference between the index and ring fingers. You do this by pulling the middle finger back out of the way, and running a straight edge along the top of the two fingers. Obviously, if the edge runs at an angle in either direction, the digits are of different lengths. The steeper the angle, the greater the imbalance between the two digits. You need to decide which digit is the longer and by how much. If the index digit is only so much as one millimeter longer than the ring digit, it's considered long. So if there's the tiniest upward slope of the straight edge toward the index digit side, it's a long index finger. If the ring finger is longer, it can be up to half a centimeter longer than the index and still be considered average. Longer than this makes it a long finger.

Check the middle finger's length next. Half the top section of the middle finger should stand higher than an imaginary line drawn across the top of the digits either side of it. If more that half the top phalange protrudes above this line, it's long. If less than half a phalange protrudes above this line, it's short.

The little finger's measure is for it to reach the top crease joint line of the ring finger beside it.

Like many palmistry skills, you'll need to measure and check the digits carefully at first. Soon though, you'll pick up an extra long or short finger with just a glance.

Traditionally (as with all palmistry features) the digits were ascribed planetary rulers. The index finger was given to the planet Jupiter, the middle digit, Saturn, the ring finger Apollo, and the

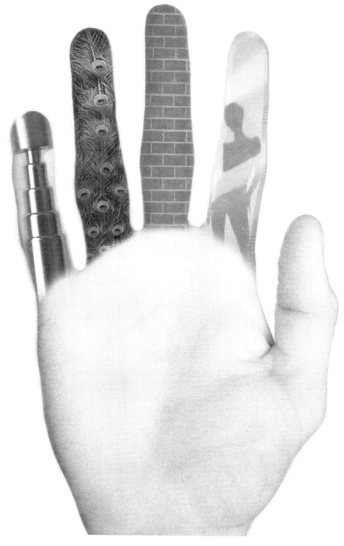

Metaphorical image of the digits

little finger Mercury. Unless you're an astrologer or into metaphorical cosmology, these labels won't mean anything. In the next few chapters, we'll make use of the more appropriate metaphors of the 'mirror' (index), the 'wall' (middle), the 'peacock' (ring) and the 'antenna' (little) finger. This will hugely help you to understand their significance.

Secret palmist assignment

You need to measure at least ten people's hands to learn how to check the finger's lengths accurately. Measure the hands of your friends and relatives, but don't feel you don't have to read their palms, yet. Look for some examples of long and short fingers, stiff and flexible fingers, and try to find a person with knotty fingers.

Brain bashing quiz
Time given: ten minutes

1. Would a short-fingered person make a good student of comparative literature?
2. Would a builder be likely to sport long fingers?
3. Does a short-fingered person have an eye for detail?
4. Would a knotty-fingered person be likely to jump to conclusions?
5. Is a stiff-fingered person relaxed and open minded?
6. Is a flexible fingered person bloody minded?
7. How is the ring finger measured?
8. How is the little finger measured?
9. Is an index finger a tiny fraction longer than the ring finger considered average?

Answers are on the next page.

HOUR FIVE
MIRRORING THE SELF – THE
INDEX FINGER

Mirror, mirror on the hand....

The index finger is by far the most important of the digits to a palmist. It's known as the mirror finger, because it's about a person's quality of self-reflection. If the finger's only the tiniest fraction longer than the ring finger, the bearer will spend long hours in self-reflection and have an exaggerated sense of themselves. If it's short (more than half a centimeter shorter than the ring finger) the person will have an undersized self-image with low self-esteem.

An average (and dismissible) size of this digit is for it to be up to half-a-centimeter shorter than the ring finger. This will mean a straight edge over the tips of these fingers would drop toward the index side slightly.

Reflecting too much

Long mirror-fingered people take themselves seriously. They're naturally bossy and intensely self-aware. If this digit is well-

Answers

1. No. Short fingered folk like less abstract and more holistic forms of knowledge.
2. No. A builder would possess short fingers.
3. No. A short fingered person has little eye for detail.
4. No. Knotty fingered people tend to be thorough and pedantic.
5. No. Stiff fingered individuals are tense physically and rigid minded.
6. No. Loose fingered people tend to be open minded and relaxed.
7. The ring finger is measured in comparison with the index digit.
8. The little finger's tip should reach the top crease line on the neighboring ring digit.
9. No. This would be considered a long index finger.

Long mirror finger on Hillary Clinton's palm

developed, research has established early development of self-reliance instigated (consciously or unconsciously) by the mother figure. A long mirror finger is more common on females than males. They were exposed to higher levels of oestrogen in the womb.

Long mirror-fingered children are reared to be the conscientious, sensible, responsible one in the family. They often assume the role of an adult at an early age. Responsibility is heaped on their shoulders by a strong, much respected, mother figure or it falls to them because of an unreliable (or absent) one.

They tend to be idealists, striving to be the best and to achieve the high standards thy set themselves in everything.

Long mirror digit people are much more likely than short mirror-fingered people to keep a diary or personal journal. They're drawn to all self-reflective pursuits: psychology, counseling, self-development, astrology – anything related to the arts of looking into themselves and by extension, into others.

The large mirror digit affords no ability to hide behind a mask and so

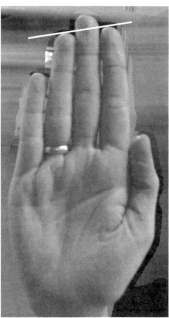

A long mirror digit

they tend to be honest and sincere, with a dislike of pretences. In appearance they tend to avoid anything flashy or ostentatious.

They need to see themselves reflected in their surroundings, so go for work that demands a strong personal input, like self-employment, people management, self development, or a mothering role, like teaching or caring. Work for them always has an emphasis on high standards, quality and ideals. They expect high rewards and appreciation, as they believe in themselves.

As a general trait, people with long mirror fingers tend to take on too much and find it hard to delegate. The long mirror gives an exaggerated sense of self and magnifies one's own flaws. Hence there can be much self-criticism, perfectionism and a perennial sense of striving.

Shrinking self-image

Where the mirror finger is short (more than half a centimeter shorter than the ring finger, so a straight edge drops sharply) the person has a poor self-image. In such cases early developmental experiences gave a notable lack of a sense of self-awareness and responsibility. This is usually through inattentive parenting skills where bad behavior or attention-seeking is rewarded or a child is given little opportunity (consciously or unconsciously) of considering their own true natures, needs and responsibilities.

A short mirror-fingered person usually compensates for their weak sense of self by hiding behind the persona which is indicated by the ring finger (obviously if the mirror is short the ring digit will be comparatively long).

This means they can often be a rather loud, jovial public person, but the private self is where their weakness lies. A short mirror-fingered person is much more likely to suffer all the illnesses of self neglect, including excessive smoking, obesity and alcoholism. They lack a sense of self worth. These people don't take themselves seriously and generally avoid responsibility, never feeling worthy of what accolades (if any) life awards them.

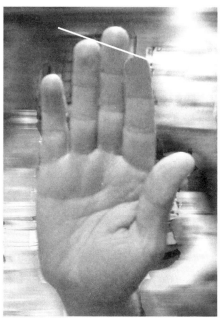

A short mirror digit

Whenever you find this finger short, always encourage the person to believe in themselves and to express their private and true needs more freely.

Bending, measuring and comparing

If this (or any finger) bends, it will weaken the finger and make it shorter. Always measure a bent finger as you would a straight one.

Always compare the mirror (index) fingers of both hands. It's nearly always slightly longer on the active hand, showing a greater sense of self-awareness and inner confidence developing as a person matures.

Secret palmist assignment

Look out for people with long and short mirror (index) fingers. You should be able to see outstanding examples easily. Try to engage anyone with an exceptionally long or short mirror finger in conversation. Ask them about their background, mother relationship and sense of inner confidence.

Brain bashing quiz
Time given: ten minutes

1. Who spends more time in self-reflection, a long or a short mirror-fingered person?
2. Does a short mirror-fingered person have confidence in themselves?
3. Is a short mirror-fingered person a perfectionist?
4. What does it say about the mother finger if the mirror digit is long?
5. Would a long mirror-fingered person be interested in psychology?
6. Is a bent mirror finger the sign of a loner?
7. Is a long mirror-fingered person likely to exhibit signs of self-neglect?
8. Would a long mirror-fingered person been likely to have indulged in attention seeking as a child?
9. Would a short mirror-fingered person have been the mature, grown up, responsible one in the family as a child?

Answers are on the next page.

HOUR SIX
WALLS, BOUNDARIES AND
CONVENTIONS – THE MIDDLE
FINGER

Going over the wall

This, the longest digit, shows our mental awareness of convention, structure, conformity and morality. It's called the wall digit, because it represents mental boundaries and our attitude to authority. It's about the qualities that keep us on the straight and narrow: career, religion, sense of society and what might be called normality.

High walls...

If the finger is long, more than half of the top section stands above a line across the tip of the ring and mirror and ring digits. When this occurs, there's a sense of taking life, work and convention seriously. The person cares a lot about rules, the law and doing the right thing.

A long wall digit person has a sense of gravitas, they feel life's

---

Answers

1. The long mirror-fingered person spends more time in self-reflection.
2. No. A short mirror-fingered person tend to doubt themselves and their abilities.
3. No. This is much more typical of a long mirror finger.
4. Responsibility was heaped on their shoulders by a strong, much respected, mother figure or it fell to them because of an unreliable (or absent) one.
5. Yes. Long mirror-fingered folk are interested in all forms of self-reflection.
6. No. A bend tends to make a finger shorter, it's measured just like a straight one.
7. No. This is much more typical of a short mirror digit.
8. No. Again, this is much more typical of a short mirror digit.
9. No. They would have avoided responsibility and not have had their sense of self reinforced.

duties and obligations upon them and are usually found within large bureaucratic structures, i.e. the church, town planning, academia, the tax office. It's fair to say this feature can make a person a bit dull. **...And short ones**

If the finger's short, or bent, the person will be unconventional, and will want to march to a different drum. They won't necessarily follow the rules and will hate ever to be seen as 'normal'.

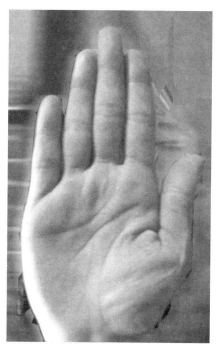

A long wall digit

A short wall digit

A short wall-fingered person is less stable mentally, they have little sense of where the boundaries of convention lie, what being sensible or doing the 'right' thing is. They're disorganized, with a tendency toward stress and depression and it's harder for them to stick at 'boring' activities (particularly careers) that lack glamour or excitement. They

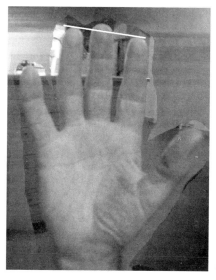

A short wall digit

Short wall digit on the palm of disgraced Enron boss, Ken Lay

are much more likely than most to bend or break the rules.

Short wall-fingered people are much more likely to follow an alternative life path. You'll find them on the hands of conspiracy theorists, followers of unconventional spiritual movements, animal rights campaigners and those that adapt well to foreign cultures and countries.

When this finger's short, the eccentric mind-set this gives can lend a zany inventiveness which is a boost to creative expression.

Mix and match

Compare the length of the wall digits on the passive and active hands. When the passive hand wall digit is longer than on the active, a person will be anti-authoritarian at work, but privately concerned with family obligations. If it's longer on the active palm, a person would have had negative experiences of family and authority as a child. However, professionally, the sense of duty, conventionality and conformism will be normal.

Secret palmist assignment

Try to find some examples of long and short wall fingers. You'll need to look particularly at the palms of outsiders, dropouts and rebels for short wall digits; and the hands of people that uphold the system: tax inspectors, government officials, for example, for long ones.

Brain bashing quiz

Time given: ten minutes

1. Why is the middle finger called the wall digit?
2. Who would be more likely to be rebellious, a long or a short wall digit person?
3. Would a short wall digit person make a good tax inspector?
4. Is a short wall-fingered person likely to follow an alternative religion?
5. Would someone with a long wall digit be a zany person?
6. Would a long wall-fingered person take work and family obligations seriously?
7. What kind of wall digit would a bureaucrat have?
8. What are the advantages of a short wall digit?
9. What does it mean if the wall finger is long on the passive hand but short on the active?

Answers are on the next page.

HOUR SEVEN
THE PEACOCK OF PERSONA –
THE RING FINGER

Strutting your stuff

This, the third, or ring finger is christened the peacock finger. This digit has traditionally been associated with the sun god, Apollo. Apollo is god of the arts and is particularly linked with the dramatic arts. This is why palmists customarily see the sign of an artist as someone with a long peacock finger.

The peacock finger is never found short. It's measured in relation to the mirror finger. You learned how to measure the difference between the two accurately in hour four, remember? When the mirror finger is the longer of the two, you only concentrate on the self-reflective qualities of the mirror digit and ignore the peacock finger.

When long, the peacock finger has been linked in several recent research papers to higher levels of testosterone. The long digit gives sporting prowess, a need for attention, flirtatiousness, higher

Answers

1. It's called the wall digit because it represents our mental awareness of convention, structure, and conformity; qualities that keep us on the straight and narrow: career, religion, sense of society rules and normality.
2. A short wall-fingered person is much more likely to rebel.
3. No. This finger being short gives little ability to apply rules and regulations.
4. Yes. Any alternative path will suit.
5. No. Long wall-fingered folk are likely to be extremely conventional.
6. Yes. These are important values to a long wall-fingered person.
7. He or she would almost certainly have a long wall digit.
8. They can posses a zany inventiveness and disregard for convention.
9. This gives a public anti-authoritarian attitude, however, at home and with family the person would be conventional and keen to obey familial conventions.

virility, a tendency for risk-taking and heightened spatial awareness.

Strutting and rutting

This research solidly proves that the peacock finger represents the measure of our genetic drive to display ourselves in a favorable light. This is a hangover from primitive times, when males of the species competed in order to win females. It is about our persona, the mask we wear as our public face. And this is why it's named the peacock finger. It gives a drive to show off, to flirt, to exhibit to others whatever skills or abilities one may have. Long peacock digits are more common on males.

It seems that women's subconscious minds are highly attracted to long peacock-fingered, testosterone-fuelled types. In a one-off experiment, ten male guinea-pigs were chosen, four of whom had long peacock fingers. A group of women took turns to hold the men's hands through a curtain and then rated them for all-round sexiness. In three different experiments, the four long peacock-fingered men came out tops.

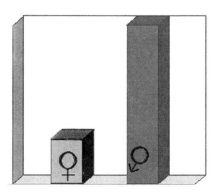

Sample graph of 10,000 male and female hands with proportion of long peacock fingers. Women's hands are represented by the column on the left.

The masculine principle

In many ways, this digit represents masculine patterns of behavior: hiding inner needs and deeper feelings behind a mask, bragging, attention-seeking, inventiveness, a love of danger and excitement. Someone with a long peacock digit will always be a little larger than life. They're likely to have good presentation skills and to possess a well-developed sense of themselves as a mythical, media or public figure.

Practically all professional entertainers, sports people, artists and celebrities have a peacock finger of exaggerated length. When the finger's *very* long, there tends to be a personal magnetism that's very attractive to the opposite sex. Bear in mind, however, that though such people may have boundless *public* confidence, their private self-esteem (as shown by a comparatively short mirror finger) will be inadequate.

Don't assume (as traditional palmists have) that merely having this finger long makes one an artist, actor, athlete or person of great talent. It only gives a drive to **Tom Cruise - check** display whatever gifts one has to the world. **out his long peacock** Don't assume you'll only find it only on **finger!** males, either.

A long peacock finger can manifest passively, as in say, owning a flashy car, having an impressive garden, adorning yourself with fourteen tattoos or as simply possessing a tendency to take risks. It can create a compulsive gambler, a bed-hopping Lothario or someone who drives too fast.

In almost every case, the peacock digit is slightly shorter on the active hand, showing less of a need for attention seeking as one matures.

Secret palmist assignment

When you watch TV or go to the movies, try to get a glimpse of the palms of your favorite stars. You'll soon see the more outrageous, risky and 'out there' the performer is, the bigger their peacock finger is.

See if you can get the prints of people you know with long peacock fingers. Probe them gently about their need for self-expression, and ask them if they hide behind the face they present to the world. Be tactful!

Brain bashing quiz
Time given: ten minutes

1. Would a long peacock-fingered person be likely to hide behind a public mask?
2. Would a long peacock-fingered person be inclined to take risks?
3. Which finger is long on the hands of celebrities? You should have no trouble with this one.
4. Is a long peacock finger a sign of artistic talent?
5. Is the long peacock finger more common on females?
6. What qualities are given by a short peacock finger?
7. Does a long peacock digit indicate higher levels of

oestrogen?

8. Is the length of this digit a sign of the primitive instinct to survive?

9. Is a ring finger half a centimeter longer than the index finger extra-long?

Answers are on the next page.

HOUR EIGHT
THE ANTENNA OF
COMMUNICATION –
THE LITTLE FINGER

Picking up the signals

This, the antenna digit is the measure of latent communication skills. Whether someone has the gift of the gab, a good vocabulary and a love of language is down to the development of this finger. It's also about financial skills and sexual communication.

The average length is for the tip to be level with the top phalange crease of the neighboring digit, but measuring this finger can be tricky if it's low-set. On a third of women and one tenth of men, the finger is set deep into the palm, so that it may look short, but is actually of normal length.

Check this by observing the first joint crease (nearest the palm) of the antenna finger – it should be level with a point half way up

Answers

1. A long peacock-fingered person would hide behind their persona. They are driven to display what talents or abilities they possess. A long mirror-fingered person can only be themselves.
2. A long peacock-fingered person would certainly be inclined to take risks. This has been proven in scientific research.
3. Celebrities invariably display a long peacock finger.
4. When this finger's long, it isn't the sign of artistic talent. It indicates a need to show off, and this may simply be by indulging in risky or reckless behavior.
5. Long peacock fingers are far more common on males than females.
6. Trick question! The peacock finger is never short. You simply read the mirror finger as being the longer and ignore this finger
7. No. It indicates higher residual levels of testosterone.
8. No. It's length is an indication of the instinct to show off, and to display skills in order to attract a mate.
9. No. This is average.

the bottom section of the peacock digit. If it is low-set, you need to add a half centimeter to its length to judge it correctly.

Long antenna

When this digit is long, like a long antenna, it receives and transmits language effectively. Its length lends a feel for language, natural eloquence and usually a good vocabulary. Often long antenna-fingered people are good with money and are somewhat shrewd. A long finger is commonly found on politicians, comedians, financial speculators, writers, teachers, sales reps and lawyers.

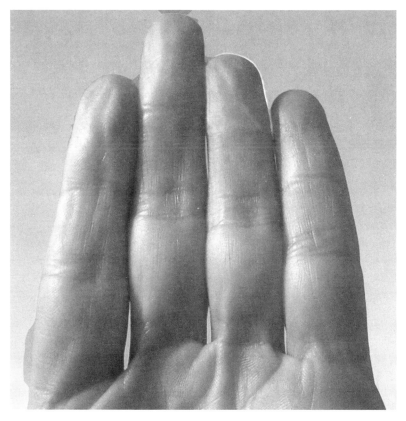

A long antenna digit on the hand of a college lecturer

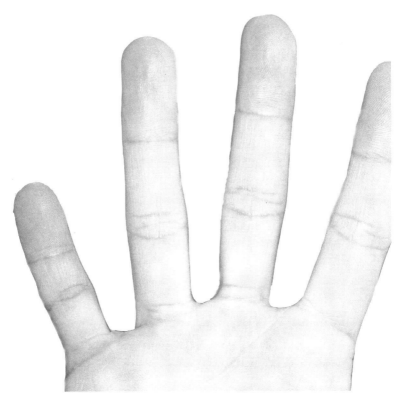

A short antenna digit

Short antenna

When the finger is short, the stunted antenna misses signals and gets overloaded easily. It's difficult to express exactly what a person feels and it's hard for them to make themselves understood. Of course, these skills can be learned and anyone with a short antenna finger should be encouraged to develop their vocabulary. A short-fingered person isn't confident using their own words, they'll be suspicious of sarcasm and irony and won't waste time reading or learning foreign languages unless absolutely necessary. They're usually insecure with personal finances.

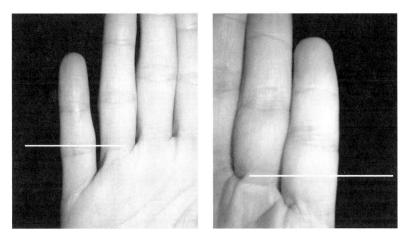

Normal and low-set antenna fingers

Low set

When this digit's low set, it's a sign that in childhood, the father figure was emotionally or physically absent, or there was an unusually close and adoring role. It's seven times more common on woman than men. It shows a deep-set under-development in sexual articulacy and a sense of sexual immaturity. Until this feature is understood, there can be confusion between sexual and emotional needs, and a seeking of a 'father (or mother in case of males) figure' in relationships. Often women and men with this sign go for much older, dominant or simply inappropriate partners.

Bending words

When this finger bends slightly

Christina Aguilera, note her low-set antenna digit

Jim Carrey's long antenna and peacock digits

towards the peacock finger there's a natural charm and seductiveness, especially if it's also long. You could say there was the ability to bend language for effect. It's also the sign of a liar or exaggerator.

If the finger sticks out, it's a sign of independence of mind, eccentricity and if on the passive hand, someone on the lookout for a sexual partner.

When both this and the peacock finger are long, wit and a good sense of humor is guaranteed.

Secret palmist assignment

If anyone you meet seems to have a certain eloquence and wit, check out the length of their antenna digits. You'll find them long in every case. Look particularly at anyone in a profession where communication is important, the finger is always long in such cases.

Brain bashing quiz

Time given: ten minutes

1. Would a writer be likely to bear a long or a short antenna finger?

2. Does a person with a short antenna digit love sarcasm?

3. What sign would you expect to see on a woman's hand that sought a 'father figure' in relationships?

4. Are people with short antenna fingers good with money?

5. Would a comedian have a short antenna digit?

6. What should you encourage a person with a short antenna digit to do?

7. How can you tell if the antenna finger is low set?

8. Is a low set antenna digit more common on men?

9. What does it mean if the antenna digit is bent?

Answers are on the next page.

HOUR NINE
PLAYING DETECTIVE –
INVESTIGATING THE
FINGERPRINTS

The devil is in the detail

You'll have noticed by now that palmistry is simply a matter of paying attention to detail. You observe a non-average feature, like a short mirror finger or a stiff thumb and from this you make penetrating insights into someone's personality. It's not difficult if you go slowly and measure each quality carefully. If you've got this far, and have completed the end-of-chapter exercises, you're well on your way to being a palmist.

The process of reading a hand is a kind of detective work, seeing a host of impressions in the smallest detail.

Now, wouldn't it be brilliant if you could look at a palm and tell how someone thinks? Well, reading the print patterns will enable you to do just that! This is where you'll need to use your magnifying glass, in classic, Sherlock Holmes style, as the print patterns can be hard to see with the naked eye.

Answers

1. A writer is likely to bear a long antenna finger
2. People with a short antenna digit are suspicious of sarcasm
3. This quality would manifest as a low-set antenna digit
4. People with short antenna digits tend to be poor with money.
5. No. Comedians invariably have long antenna digits.
6. Advise them to learn to communicate more effectively.
7. It's low set if the first crease of this finger is level with the base of the pea cock digit.
8. No. Low set antenna digits are much more common on women.
9. A bent antenna digit gives charm and the ability to manipulate language for effect.

The power of the print patterns

The prints (found on the fingertips and on the palm itself) have become hugely important in palmistry over the last fifty years. Reading the prints adds an extra layer to a palm analysis that brings out a person's deeper thinking processes. Thousands of research papers have been published on finger and palm prints as genetic indicators of personality traits and predispositions to particular illnesses.

The prints' particular formations tell us the genetically-inherited manner in which an individual processes information. They don't tell us *what* a person is thinking, but the *way* in which they think. In this chapter, we'll look at the meaning of the various types of pattern. In the next, we'll go back to the fingers and thumb and read any notable prints on them.

The prints are formed by multiple lines of skin ridges (we looked at the skin ridges on the palm in the second chapter). The scientific name for the prints is rather scary and long-winded: 'dermatoglyphics', which is from the Greek for 'skin carvings'.

The best way to think about dermatoglyphics is as formations representing brain waves. The shape and form of the print shows the shape and form of the mental field in a particular area of the mind. The prints are like the arrangements of brain synapses, making us think in a particular habitual way. The prints never change, they indicate the fixed and permanent manner in which people process information. The various loops, swirls, circles and chevron formations show the prevailing mental wavelength a person is on.

You must relate the print pattern to the part of the hand you find it on. For instance, the print pattern on the mirror finger tells you about the way a person processes thoughts about themselves, while the print on the antenna finger tells you about the mental wavelength a person is on in terms of communication. Confused? You won't be, after we've covered the prints in more detail.

The seven print patterns

Though every print pattern on every person you meet will be unique, they all fall into one of seven basic formations. We'll go through them one at a time with the commonest first and the rarest last.

Common loops

By far the most widespread pattern is the common loop. Common loops look like a cross-section of a wave of water moving across the ocean. The wave crest flows toward the thumb side of the palm. They represent a sense of going with the flow, someone that needs to belong, to be part of the social current.

The loop shows a responsive nature, someone who moves easily from one mood, one person, one place to another. The loop is a mental pattern of sociability, connecting, resonating with the prevailing tide. The loop is about fitting in, and to a great extent, being normal. The loop is so common it is considered to be average and the good news is, whenever you find one of these on the fingers you can ignore it as it's unremarkable.

The exception to this is when you find what's called a *radial*

Loop prints

loop. This is a rarer type of loop where the loop is thrown away from the thumb side of the palm towards the antenna finger side.

Radial loop

Whenever you find a radial loop on a digit this is remarkable and

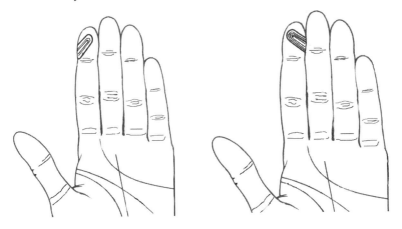

Radial loop   **Common loop**

will affect the person's consciousness strongly. The radial loop indicates such an extreme mental state of openness to others that they lose sight of their own desires. Radial loops create a compulsion to prioritize others needs over one's own, and an insecure, unstable, hyper-responsive personality.

Simple Arch

The chevron lines of the simple arch resemble layers of soil, repressing, burying, and fixing in place. The simple arch pattern makes an individual practical, cautious, repressed, fixed, materialistic, physical, stubborn, loyal and old-fashioned. Usually this pattern gives physical skills and a love of working with the hands.

On the rare occasions where you find eight or more of the

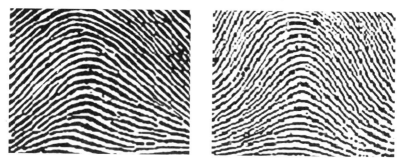

Simple arches

fingers all bearing this pattern, the person is highly repressed and unable to adapt to the modern world. Simple arches are found on all those that get stuck in patterns of behavior, and those that believe in ancient value systems. Though one or two of these patterns on a palm makes someone careful and shows a need for security, someone with a lot of simple arches, say four or more on one palm, is actually rebellious, reacting to what they see as the slick superficiality and unhealthy modernity of the world.

Whorl

The whorl pattern looks like a bulls-eye with concentric rings around the centre. Similarly, the whorl creates a mind-set of highly targeted thought patterns, someone that can shut the world out and focus on just one particular subject or idea. Whorls often mean the development of a skill or specialty, especially if there are four or more on the fingertips. It's also a strong indicator of individuality and a love of freedom. A whorled person likes to create a lot of space around themselves. A lot of whorls on the fingers can make a person inclined to be a strongly focused, inventive and somewhat obsessive personality.

People with whorls are secretive, original, and usually highly motivated. The greater the number of whorls there are on the fingertips, the more a person is given to oddness, alienation, the development of talents, and the need for space.

Whorl prints

Peacock's eye

A variation on the whorl is the above pattern, known as a peacock's eye. It's still a whorl, but as it's within a loop, it's a little less obvious.

The rule is, if there's a set of circles or a spiral in the pattern, it's classed as a whorl.

Peacock's eye

Composite

The next in our list is the composite print. It's made up of two loops going in opposite directions. As you might expect, it makes for a mind-set going in opposite directions, creating two viewpoints. The composite creates psychological cycles of enthusiasm and disappointment, where one is never fully able to make one's mind up on the bigger issues of life. It can be hard to see things through with this variable mind set.

Composite patterns are common on counselors, as this pattern gives a wonderful ability to see things from other people's perspective. They have a mentality that's never more absolutely certain on any point, an openness to explore options, an anti-fanatic, universal view.

Composite prints

Tented Arches

We're getting pretty low down on our list of print types. So you know these patterns are rare. Less than one percent of fingers have a tented arch on them. It looks a bit like a simple arch, except that the peak of the arch is much higher.

A tented arch throws a spike pattern sharply skyward. Think of it as a high peak on an electrocardiogram reading and you'll get the idea. It gives a highly excitable tendency, fanaticism, a need to go

Tented arches

to extremes. Tented arches create an excess of enthusiasm and excitement.

Unlocking the inner person

You can help people to understand themselves and their inner natures though explaining any unusual dermatoglyphics. The effect of having your deepest thought patterns revealed to you can be an astounding, life-enhancing and liberating experience. Try always to be positive when talking about print patterns to anyone you read for.

The next step in the easy-peasy process of print reading is to go through each notable pattern on each of the fingers. In the following chapter we'll do just that. Then we'll cover the prints on the palm itself.

Secret palmist assignment

You need to be able to recognize the various patterns, so read through the chapter once again. Make sure you know, for example, what a simple arch looks like and what it means. Study your own fingertips for any patterns that aren't common loops. You'll need to start taking some prints of palms now, so you can examine them in private without any pressure. Take ten people's hand prints - look for examples of people with a lot of whorls, and people with a lot of simple arches. See if what you know about the person coincides with what you know about these patterns.

Brain bashing quiz
Time given: ten minutes

1. How important is a common loop?

2. Does a radial loop make for a strong personality?

3. Is a person with a lot of whorls a highly social, open person?

4. What pattern indicates the likelihood of the development of talents?

5. Which pattern indicates stubbornness?

6. Which pattern indicates the likelihood of the development of manual skills?

7. Would a person with composites be decisive?

8. Would a person with a tented arch be calm and unexcitable?

9. Is a peacock's eye a kind of loop?

Answers are on the next page.

HOUR TEN
PERSONALITY PROFILING –
THE PRINTS ON THE DIGITS

Fingering the prints

We're going to go back over the thumb and fingers now, exploring the meaning of interesting print patterns you may find on any individual digit. This may seem a lot to take in, but it's not so bad if you've remembered the basics from the previous chapter. Here we'll apply what we know about a person's mental wavelength (indicated by the prints) to the various parts of the mind (as indicated by the digits).

Any finger or thumb you examine is most likely to have a common loop on it. When this is the case, ignore it. It's only exceptional patterns you're looking for. When you seen a print that's not a common loop, it's effect is always significant.

The most important print is the one on the mirror finger, because that's about a person's mind-set regarding their self-reflection. How a person thinks about themselves has a powerful

---

Answers

1. A common loop isn't important in analysis, it's ignored.
2. Radial loops make a person insecure in themselves and hyper-receptive to others influence.
3. Lots of whorls on the palm make a person individualistic, freedom loving, intense and highly focused. They tend not to be the most sociable of people.
4. The focus that lots of whorls bring to a subject means they are often highly talented.
5. Simple arches impart stubbornness.
6. Simple arches often have a skilled pair of hands.
7. Composite prints give a difficulty in making decisions.
8. Tented arches make a person highly excitable and intense.
9. A peacock's eye is a type of whorl pattern.

effect on their character. We'll look at this finger first.

Mirror finger's print pattern

Whorl Someone with a whorl on the mirror finger has a strong sense of themselves as an individual, with a tendency towards secrecy, single-mindedness and a need for space.

They find it difficult to take orders from others and can be guilty of shutting others out. Often a person with this pattern will find an interest or specialty where they can operate unhindered. They like to work alone or unsupervised.

Simple arch This pattern on the mirror finger is the sign of a cautious, stubborn mind-set. They'll be unpretentious, self-effacing and reliable, putting great value on loyalty. Often folk with this pattern posses a skilled pair of hands.

They tend to block their feelings, be a touch old-fashioned and somewhat skeptical of anything new. They love directness in speech and find change difficult, easily getting trapped in cycles of behavior.

Radial loop This indicates a hyper-receptive personality. Someone whose sense of self is weak, insecure and easily lost. They often identify others' needs as their own. This quality is exaggerated if the mirror finger is also short. On a long finger this pattern can make a person a touch paranoid.

This marking is found on care workers and 'people' people who  are super-nice and ultra-friendly. They find criticism difficult to cope with; they also struggle to say 'no' to anyone. On the positive side, a radial-looped mirror finger person has the ability to 'tune in' to the moods of others. They have the gift of openness and sensitivity, so tend to be particularly popular and well-liked.

Good advice is for them to spend more time alone and to learn to say 'no'.

Composite This pattern gives uncertainly about who one really is. Life decisions are often left to the demands of the situation or to the influence of parents or a partner, rather than what one actually wants. A person with this sign can't make their mind up about their personal needs. Often they're happier living out two separate sides of their character rather than finding a fixed role. There's a gift for impartiality and diplomacy which they should be encouraged to develop.

Tented arch A tented arch on the mirror finger indicates an intense personality, someone that takes everything a little too far. This gives a sense of 'over the top' ideals, with a drive to change the world and themselves in some powerful way. Often this sign is seen in those that entertain, teach, or motivate others. People with this pattern need to learn to relax and to put their energies in challenging, life-changing activities.

The thumb's print pattern

Next in priority is the thumb print, that's about our mental approach to doing things. You could read only the print on the mirror fingers and thumbs, as they're far and away the most important. However, there may not be anything interesting on these two digits, so you may have to explore the rest of the fingers. The thumb and the remaining fingers display less variety in the prints found on them than the mirror digit. Only the patterns you're likely to find on them are given here.

Whorl This gives a drive to act independently, someone

who'll apply themselves to projects or interests that are often unconventional. Whorl-thumbed people have no problem in acting on their own initiative and love personal freedom. They have an innate need to demonstrate their independence and often find new ways of doing things.

Simple arch This signals a stubborn, practical way of approaching life goals; someone whose actions are directed pragmatically, for familial or financial ends. They'll be thorough, stubborn and persistent in action.

Composite The two-way current of the composite on the thumb creates a two-way mind-set, with an inconsistent, vacillating attitude to action.

They can have difficulty in deciding on an overall life plan and  may never be certain of their goals or know what they want to do. They alternate between enthusiasm and doubt. It's hard to be decisive with such a pattern, but it adds a considered, multi-viewed outlook that's always sympathetic to others' opinions.

People with composite thumbs should be advised that for them to be only 60% certain of anything is enough to go ahead. They can never be 100% committed to anything.

The wall finger's print pattern

This finger's dermatoglyphic, shows the way we think about values, lifestyle and work.

Whorl Values will be highly original, with a disregard of dogma and rules. They're likely to have odd or unusual beliefs and lifestyles, and to choose freedom over worldly success. There's always either an unusual job or hobby, and they'll follow a non-traditional spiritual path.

Simple arch An arch print here shapes views on work and belief systems into simple, pragmatic, old-fashioned patterns. They have a sense of duty and like order, method and fairness in the values they follow.

Justice is important. The vocational drive is towards a secure,

serious, financially rewarding position and a stable lifestyle.

Radial loop The sense of cultural identity and values will be insecure. A person with this sign will be able to adapt to different lifestyles, careers and cultures easily. They will be either over-conformist or alternative and may move between the two. They're strongly conscious of their obligations to family and authority.

Composite A composite here will cast doubt about where someone stands in terms of spirituality, values and job choice.

They suffer continual anxiety about finding the correct career, religion or belief system and are open to all.

The peacock finger's print pattern

The pattern on this digit indicates the mental approach to self-expression.

Whorl This signifies individual tastes in creativity, dress, music and the arts. A sense of perspective is indicated, with good

spatial awareness and a flair for design.

Always this pattern gives a good 'eye' for line, form and color, also originality in self expression.

Simple arch This indicates that self expression is somewhat physical. A person with this sign often needs to exercise to express themselves through the body. There's a love of archaic skills and traditional art forms, i.e. stained glass window making. Aesthetically, there's a love of historic and classical ideals of beauty.

Tented arches, composites and radial loops are extremely rare here.

The antenna finger's print pattern

This print tells us about the mental wavelength a person is on in terms of communication.

Whorl This is a rare sign and shows a love of 'insider' knowledge and language in a specialized field. People with this sign will be drawn to the mysterious workings of, for example, astrology, ancient Greek or conceptual art. They often go for unconventional intimate relationships.

Simple Arch This is again rare, and shows someone that is careful and cautious in speech.

They love to explain and break down language into its component parts, as in, for instance, speech therapy, or etymology. They are deeply inhibited in personal intimacy.

Mind reading

You can see that the basic meaning of each pattern is the same, but it varies slightly according to where it's placed. Get to know the print patterns, learn what each means for each finger.

The prints explain the complexity of human nature. When you find, for instance, a person with a composite on their thumb (uncertainty about actions, indecisive about major life issues) and a whorl on their mirror finger (independence, originality) you have a person who's determined to be independent, but is unable to decide the best course of action to achieve their goals. The more interesting print patterns a person has, the more unusual their character.

Take your time when examining prints. Try comparing the passive and active hands. Sometimes you'll find astonishing differences. There may be, for instance, a radial loop on the passive mirror finger and a whorl on the active mirror digit. This will mean that passively, in childhood, and at home with family and intimates, a person would be insecure, desperate to please and hyper-responsive. In their working life however, and in their mature, outer personality, they'll be strongly independent, unconventional and able to act on their own initiative.

It's these kind of deep personality traits that can be revealed with an understanding of the dermatoglyphics.

Secret palmist assignment

Take half-a-dozen people's hand prints and study their print patterns in private. Write down the meanings of the particular prints on the fingers and present them to your sample audience.

Brain bashing quiz
Time given: ten minutes

1. Is a radial-looped mirror finger person assertive?
2. Is a person with a whorl on their wall digit conformist?
3. What does it mean to have a simple arch on the thumb?

4. What pattern on the peacock finger is best for an artist?

5. Is a person with a simple arch on their mirror finger likely to become 'stuck' in life?

6. What work do people with tented arches on the mirror fingers often do?

7. Does a person with a composite on the wall digit have clear ideas about their work, spirituality and values?

8. What print pattern are you most likely to find on the peacock digit of someone that loves archaic art forms and traditional skills?

9. Would a person with a whorl on their antenna finger be drawn to unconventional relationships?

Answers are on the next page.

HOUR ELEVEN
PALMAR KARMA – THE PRINT
PATTERNS ON THE PALM

Markings on the body of the palm

We'll finish off the print patterns in this chapter by covering the patterns on the palm itself. Everyone has a set of prints on their fingertips, but it's relatively common to have no print patterns on the palm at all.

First of all, we'll take a look the various areas of the palm. This will be useful, not only for any dermatoglyphics you may find, but also to help you understand the meaning of the lines when we go on to them. Just like the fingers, the print pattern (or line, or other marking) is easy to interpret if you understand the meaning of the part of the palm it's on.

The body of the palm is split into four quadrants or zones. Try to memorize the meanings of the various zones.

The **World Stage** zone relates to the outer world, other people, and social connections. Whenever you see a print pattern,

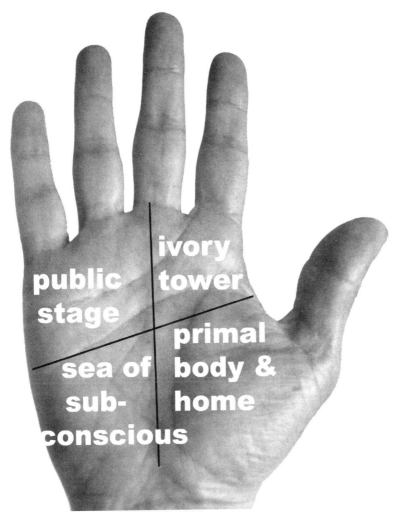

The palm map with its four zones

line or marking on this area it will influence the way a person communicates or connects with others.

The area known as the **Ivory Tower** is about ambition, self-improvement, possessions, personal influence and power.

The **Sea of Subconscious** covers the subterranean depths of the mind, the psyche, the deep 'well' of dreams, emotions and latent impulses.

The **Primal Home and Body** area holds within it the fleshy thumb ball mound you measured in the first chapter for vitality. This zone is about primal energy, the body, the home and the family. Any prints or lines here will influence a person's experience of the domestic and physical areas of life.

Interpreting the palm prints

OK, now we'll explore the meaning of any palm print patterns you may find. Remember, many hands won't have any prints here at all. Most of the patterns you do discover will be located in the Sea of Subconscious zone.

The first two patterns are found on the World Stage zone, so they affect our relationship with the outer world.

Loop of leisure

Any loop that's found between the digits links them together and exaggerates the digit's qualities. In this case, the antenna and

peacock digits are bound by a loop. The effect is to heighten the pleasure principle which is part of the expression of the peacock finger. It makes a person prioritize their leisure time. They often enthusiastically pursue a

Loop of leisure

hobby or craft and

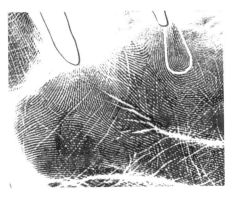

Loop of industry

they'll crave exciting holidays. Sometimes they make their leisure pursuit their profession.

With this sign, enjoyment of the work you do comes before career prospects and financial reward.

Loop of industry

This is the opposite to the previous pattern. Here the self-expressive drive of the peacock finger is bound to the more serious concerns of the wall digit. This makes a person take their work seriously. Their career and general industriousness are a kind of pleasure

Usually the drive for fun and creativity is repressed in favor of hard work.

Loop of leadership

This sign is uncommon. It links the self-reflective mirror digit with the structured wall digit on the Ivory Tower part of the palm.

It gives natural organizational ability and the knack of acquiring status or respect within a group.

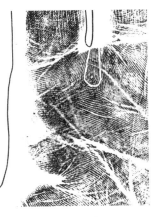

We'll move down to the Sea of **Loop of leadership**

Subconscious now, where the majority of print patterns are found. Any marking here will affect the deep well of the psyche.

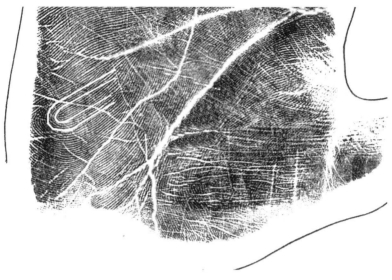

Loop of sensitivity

Loop of sensitivity

A loop here gives an awareness of the subtle currents that move just below the surface of life. Someone with this loop may perceive that you're hiding something, for instance, or may get a sense of déjà vu. Psychic perception is often possible.

This pattern also gives artistic responsiveness.

Whorl of isolation

This rare sign brings intensity to the subconscious. A person with this marking is always fascinated by dreams, psychology, spiritual evolvement or the deeper realms of the mind. It's hard for them to become emotionally close to another; they tend to have a part of themselves that holds back. A whorl in the Sea of Subconscious always gives a unique artistic vision, particularly in the dramatic arts.

Anyone with this marking can tend to get trapped inside themselves, or trapped outside their deeper natures. Always advise art as therapy for such people.

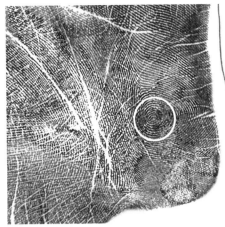

Whorl of isolation

Loop of nature

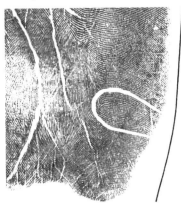

Loop of nature

A loop opening outwards anywhere along the lower edge of the Sea of Subconscious zone opens the area to natural forces. It's a sure sign of receptivity to the earth's energies and a love of nature.

With this loop, a person *must* be near growing things. It can give a gift for dowsing and healing, also a feel for energypoints in the body and in the Earth.

Composite on Sea of Subconscious

This unusual sign is rarely seen; it churns up the subconscious. The individual can experience constant emotional ups and downs, with confusion about what they really feel. There can be difficulty in maintaining a stable emotional bond and rocky relationships are often the result.

The study of gender, sexuality and psychology are often issues in this person's life.

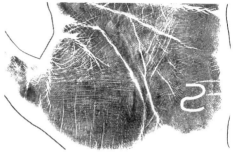

Composite on Sea of Subconscious

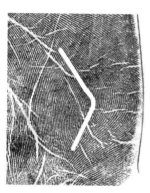

Arch on Sea of Subconscious

Arch on Sea of Subconscious

This unusual indication represses the subconscious. It makes a personality that never talks about their deeper needs and drives.

The build-up of internal pressures means they need to let off steam physically. It's common on midwives, masseurs and care workers who practically demonstrate their affections.

Loop of inspiration

This is an uncommon sign. It looks like a fountain of lines rising from the base of the palm. It creates a spout of inspiration flowing into the subconscious.

It's common on artists

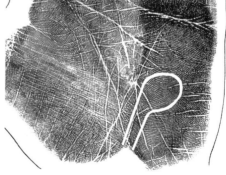

Loop of inspiration

and musicians, spiritual seekers and those fascinated by and open to mystical experiences.

Loop of rhythm

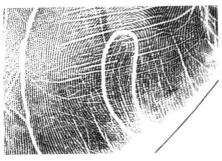

This loop in the Primal Home and Body zone gives a physical sense of rhythm and a love of music.

It's not necessarily a sign of musical talent, but musicians and dancers very often have this marking.

Loop of rhythm

Loop of courage

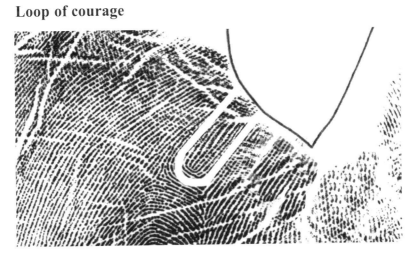

Loop of courage

The loop of courage is found at the junction between the Primal Home and Body and the Ivory Tower quadrants, in the web of skin above the thumb. It's found on those who need to set themselves challenges.

Usually, there's a lot of drive and energy about such people. They need to dare themselves, be it in riding a motorcycle or taking up karate.

Secret palmist assignment

Take another look at your hand prints from the last chapter and study them again for prints on the palm. When you find a marking, write the meaning down and relate it to the owner(s) of the respective hands.

Brain bashing quiz
Time given: ten minutes

1. What do markings on the Sea of Subconscious relate to?

2. Is a person with a loop of leisure likely to devote their life to their job?

3. Is a person with a loop of inspiration artistic?

4. What do markings on the Ivory Tower zone of the palm relate to?

5. Which palm print represses the subconscious?

6. Which palm print energizes and isolates the subconscious?

7. Which palm print gives possible psychic awareness and sensitivity?

8. Which print gives a love of nature?

9. Does a loop of rhythm make one a musician?

Answers are on the next page.

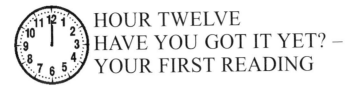

HOUR TWELVE
HAVE YOU GOT IT YET? –
YOUR FIRST READING

Read 'em and weep

As a reward for all the hard work you've put in so far, you're going to attempt your first reading! Scary isn't it? However, I think you'll be surprised at how much you've already learned. You can always flick back through these pages for reference if you get stuck.

We're going to examine the hand print of Josh, a 36 years old, right-hander. Note that the print patterns have been highlighted to make them clearer. Josh has averagely flexible thumbs and fingers and an average-sized thumb-ball mount. As you know, we dismiss anything average so we'll ignore these. His palm skin quality is silk. Examine the hand carefully while you answer the following questions. You'll be directed to what to look for in the palm in response to each question.

Start with the skin and plunge straight in...

We'll begin our reading by talking about what kind receptivity Josh

---

Answers

1. Any marking in this area affects the subconscious, the psyche, the deep 'well' of dreams, emotions and impulses.
2. No. This pattern will give an attitude of not wanting to take work too seriously.
3. This print means they could be and often are.
4. This area is about the realm of ambitions, possessions and personal power.
5. A simple arch in the Sea of Subconscious.
6. A whorl print in the Sea of Subconscious.
7. A loop of sensitivity.
8. A loop of nature.
9. The loop of rhythm gives a natural sense of rhythm and is often found on musicians.

has. Is he sensitive to his environment or thick skinned? What kind of surroundings would he thrive in? You'll need to check the skin quality to find out; also, look for a loop of sensitivity.

Now, what can you say about Josh's self-esteem? Is he bossy? What kind of parenting experience did he have? Look at the length of the mirror finger first; see if it's long or short in relation to the

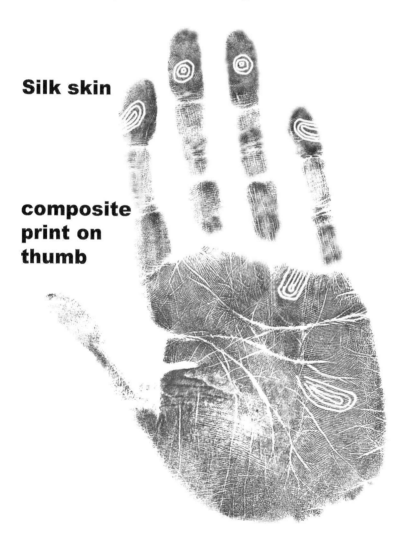

Silk skin

composite print on thumb

peacock finger. Then add the qualities of the print pattern on the mirror finger to your findings. This will tell you his how he thinks about himself.

How are you doing? Not so very difficult is it? The key is not to rush, and to try to milk all you know from each point.

Motivation and self-discipline are vital in achieving goals. Also, it's difficult to attain anything unless we have will power. Look at Josh's thumb. It's of average length and stiffness, but what does the print pattern on it tell you about his attitude to life goals?

It's Josh's rebelliousness or conformity we'll look at next. You'll need to examine the wall finger for this. Which is he? The wall digit's print pattern will tell you what he seeks from the work he does. The finger's length is average, and therefore forgettable, but the print on it certainly isn't. What does this print tell you? Expanding on the work issue, look also for a loop of industry, is there one present?

Now for self-expression. Does Josh have a need to express himself? Does he hide behind the mask of a persona? Look at the length of the peacock finger. His attitudes to this issue will be found in the print on it. Check also for a loop of leisure. This is important, because it makes a person prioritize their leisure pursuits.

Now we'll check out his communication skills. The antenna finger is examined for this. Josh's antenna finger is actually long. It looks short because it's low set. What does both the length and the low setting tell you?

Summing up

OK, how have you done? All the answers are in Appendix 2 at the back of this book. Go over your responses to the questions again and then look at the answers.

Remember, this has only been a 'quickie' reading. We've only gone over the main points and yet you've hopefully unearthed some crucial insights into Josh's personality. This kind of information would stagger anyone whose palm you read.

We obtained all this information by looking at the active hand only. If we read *both* palms we'd learn even more. We could then check the difference between every feature on the palms and measure the difference between the inner and outer personalities.

Congratulations on your fine work. Well done!

Secret palmist assignment

Take the prints of five people and work through them, starting with the skin texture and covering all the points you've learned so far. Then present the points you've uncovered to the people whose hand prints you've taken. Note their reactions.

You know enough now to make powerful insights into anyone's personality. At this, the half-way point of this book, take a breather. Go back over all the chapters. Make sure you've learned all there is to say about the skin texture, the fingers and the print patterns before you proceed.

Brain bashing quiz
Time given: ten minutes

1. What feature tells us about Josh's receptivity?
2. What do you look at in Josh's palm to give clues about his self-esteem?
3. Does the print pattern on the mirror digit tell you how Josh thinks about other people?
4. What does the thumb have to do with achieving life goals?
5. Does the wall digit's length tell you about Josh's drive to express himself in art and creativity?
6. Does the print pattern on the peacock finger show Josh's attitude to himself?
7. Does Josh's have a loop of nature?
8. Does Josh have a simple arch on his peacock digit?
9. Does Josh have a loop of industry?

Answers are on the next page.

HOUR THIRTEEN
MIND MAPPING – THE MAJOR LINES

The big four

The major lines are the four most prominent lines you'll find on anyone's palm. Two of them (the Line of Emotion and the Line of Consciousness) begin at opposite sides of the palm and move horizontally across its surface. A third line (the Vitality Line) starts above the thumb and curves downward around the thumb ball. The last one (the Lifepath Line) starts at the bottom of the palm and moves up through the centre towards the wall digit.

The major lines always begin in the same place, but vary hugely in where they end.

Take a look at your own hand and see if you can identify these four lines. They may be longer or shorter than the ones in the illustration and may bend more or be straighter than the ones shown. The Lifepath Line is probably the weakest and shortest of your major lines.

---

answers

1. The quality of the skin texture is the measure of receptivity.
2. The length of the mirror digit comparative to the peacock finger.
3. No. The print on this digit is about his attitude to himself.
4. The thumb shows will power, self control and attitude to attainments. These are all vital in achieving life goals.
5. No. The wall digit's length tells you about the drive for convention, career and conformism.
6. No. The peacock finger's print tells you about the prevailing attitude to self-expression and display.
7. No. There is a loop of sensitivity present, but not a loop of nature.
8. No. There is a whorl on this digit.
9. No. There is a loop of leisure, but not a loop of industry.

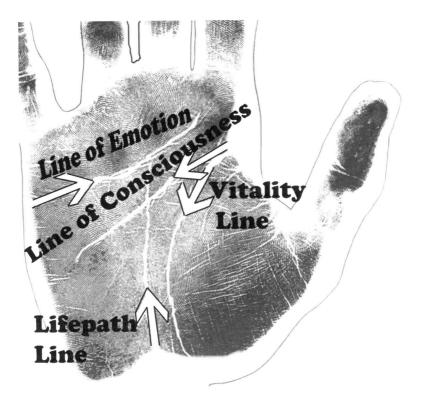

The major lines

If any of the major lines seem to be missing or only partially formed, don't panic! You aren't about to die young, nor are you some kind of weirdo. We'll look at these issues in more detail when we examine the lines individually in the next few chapters.

Other, less prominent lines (known as the minor lines) may or may not be present.

Changing lines, changing times

The lines form in the womb at around the third month and they change throughout your lifetime. Take a look at the following before and after images. This is the palm of someone before and after electro- convulsive therapy.

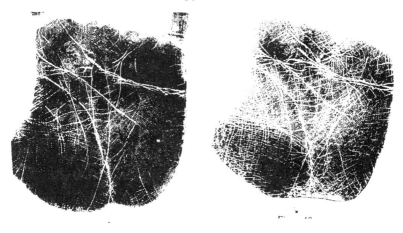

Before ECT treatment   **After ECT treatment**

You can see from these images that the lines can change very rapidly indeed. Can there possibly be any doubt that the palm represents brain function?

The first thing to say about the lines is that you can tell a great deal simply by looking at their quality. A set of deep, red lines show a person with deep, passionate energy coursing through them. Weak, faded lines show someone more tentative and considered in their actions, with less 'oomph'.

Full or empty, bold or feeble?

A palm covered with hundreds of fine lines is known as a 'full' hand. This indicates a stressful, complex, highly strung, nervous person.

A palm with only a few clear lines on it is called an 'empty' hand. This is a much less complex and more focused

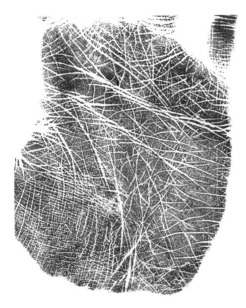

Full hand

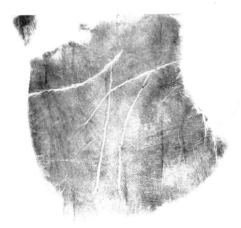

Empty hand

personality, who likes life to be straightforward and uncomplicated.

As a general rule, the finer the skin quality, the more lines you're likely to see.

The major lines show the way a person experiences the world. If someone has a set of lines that are chained, full of dots and breaks, their experiences are incoherent. To them, life will be a chain of muddled and unstable situations.

A person with clear, bold lines will be able to make sense of things and order their experiences.

The lines on the palm are like tracks marked by repetitively thinking along the same lines. When the patterns of our minds change, so the lines change. However unclear a person's lines are, they can and often do, improve considerably over time.

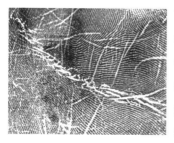

Poor-quality line

Up, down and across

Crudely speaking, vertical lines (if well formed and clear) are about a sense of holding on, going deeper, getting better, improving the quality of life, inner development, extending skills and self knowledge and staying fixed on course. Horizontal lines are about power over the exterior world, shaping, owning, ordering, conceiving, and connecting to people, places and possessions.

It's interesting that on engravings of ancient hands there are an abundance of vertical lines, where on modern palms the opposite is true. This indicates a withdrawal from inner realms over time to the outer world of the present, in a more material, less spiritual culture.

What to look for

As a palmist, the golden rule of 'ignore the average' applies just as much to the lines as to any other palm feature. If a line is of average length, strength and form, there's only so much that can be said about it. It's much more interesting when a line is distinguished by being too long or short, or it has a break or some other marking on it. This represents a distinctive, individual experience that is hugely important to the person whose hand you're looking at.

When you look at the major lines, always check to see which is the strongest. Ideally it's the Vitality Line. The Vitality Line is about our ability to be stable and to have sufficient energy. If it's not the strongest line, a person's stability is dependant on their emotions, their life goals or their ideas (depending on which other line is the stronger). This makes them more vulnerable to upheavals than they could be.

Next, look at the length of the major lines. If any line completely crosses the palm from side to side or top to bottom, it

Complete crossing line

always creates a highly repressed and obsessive personality.

If, alternatively, a major line travels less than a third of the height or width of the palm, a person has a limited ability in a given area.

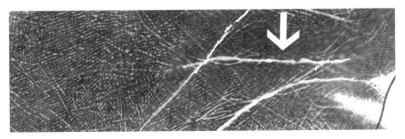

Short line

Interruptions, disruptions and other strange happenings

Breaks, bars, dots and islands are interruptions in a person's life experience. It's all too easy to get fixated with these more subtle markings, but you can safely ignore them if they're not clearly marked.

Breaks

A break in a line shows something ending – a relationship or family situation, or job or personality trait. A break in a line with a clear gap makes a person vulnerable to some kind of breakdown and possibly illness. If there's a break halfway down the Line of Emotion, for instance (this line shows emotional experiences) a person will have suffered an interruption of their ability to feel and connect to others. Not only will this be felt in their *day-to-day* experiences, but the marking can also be *measured along the line chronologically*. It will refer to a particular incident half way through their life. Therefore, we can roughly time past events from where a marking is. Where a break (or crossing line or any marking) is indicated further along a line at a point somewhere in the future, don't see this as a prediction of an event. As the years progress, the marking may change or vanish altogether. If anything, see it as a sign the person needs to take a good look at themselves and make some changes, so that the character traits represented by the marking don't continue and create problems.

Break in the Line of Emotion

Complete breaks (with a gap between the two ends of a line) are rare. More often than not, there's an overlap where the line restarts alongside the break.

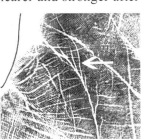

Overlap

An overlap shows a point in life where some-one stops a pattern of behavior and starts again, often into better levels of experience (if the line becomes clearer and stronger after the overlap).

Branches

Fine lines or branches that run upwards off the main lines toward the fingers show idealism and positive attitudes and events.

Rising lines

Fine lines or branches that plunge downwards from the main lines are linked to a depression, loss, draining energy and nega-tive events.

Falling lines

Doubled lines

Sometimes a line is doubled and this means a kind of double life - two sets of needs, or two layers of personality in the realm the line refers to. If it's the Vitality Line, for instance, a person is likely to have two homes, two bases, two lifestyles and a lot of energy.

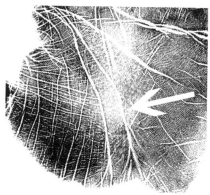

Doubled line

Dots

Dots represent a flare of energy, a point where a person has become worked up, angry or excited over a particular issue.

Islands

Islands are always negative. They indicate stress and confusion.

A dot

An island

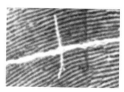

A bar line

Bar lines

A fine line crossing a major line is called a bar line. This represents a person or set of circumstances that interrupts a person's progress. This tends to take energy and time to sort out.

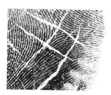

A square

Squares

Squares show times of restriction and responsibility, where someone is working through a tough time but developing new skills and resources.

Secret palmist assignment

Pick out the major lines on your own palm and make yourself familiar with them. Note which is your strongest line. Note the major line's beginnings and endings. Look for examples of breaks, overlaps, islands and bar lines. Look for the major lines on the prints in your collection. Look for examples of 'full hands' and 'empty hands', look for any interesting markings.

Brain bashing quiz
Time given: ten minutes

1. What does it mean if a person has a 'full hand'?
2. And an 'empty hand'?
3. When a line crosses the palm completely from side-to-side, what kind of person does this indicate?
4. What does a complete break in a line signify?
5. What does a break and an overlap in a line tell you?
6. What does a doubled line mean?
7. If there are small lines rising up off a major line, what do they mean?
8. What does a bar line crossing a major one indicate?
9. What about islands? Are their effects positive?

Answers are on the next page.

HOUR FOURTEEN
ROOTS, GROUNDING AND
ENERGY – THE VITALITY LINE

A matter of life and death?

This line (traditionally called the lifeline) makes everyone nervous, because of its customary association with predictions of an early death.

This line is the measure of stability and vitality. Breaks and markings on this line represent major changes in stability. The length of the line represents available energy. In medieval times, any change was bad, usually fatal. No-one won the lottery, got a salary increase or went to college. Any change marked on this line was likely to be in the form of war, disease or famine and this is where the connection with disaster and death began.

Power line

Imagine this line as a root that draws up energy stored in the thumb

---

Answers

1. A 'full hand' indicates a stressful, highly strung, nervous person.
2. An empty hand has very few lines on it. It shows a highly focused personality
3. A line that completely crosses the palm always indicates an obsessive that lacks complexity.
4. A break in a line with a gap makes a person vulnerable to some kind of personality.
5. An overlap shows a point in life where someone stops a pattern of behavior breakdown and possibly illness.
6. Doubled lines mean two levels of experience, two layers of personality in the and starts again, often into better levels of experience.
7. Rising lines show idealism, optimism and positive events. realm the lines refer to.
8. Bar lines are obstacles that interrupt progress.
9. No. Islands indicate stress and confusion.

ball mound (do you remember checking this out in Chapter One?). This root moves energy through the internal organs. It stabilizes and fixes a person in place, giving them a sense of security and permanence.

Shallow roots, weak roots

If the Vitality line is short, a person is much more likely to move around and be rootless in life. They'll be insecure; a stable job or marriage may give them structure but they can't create stability for themselves.

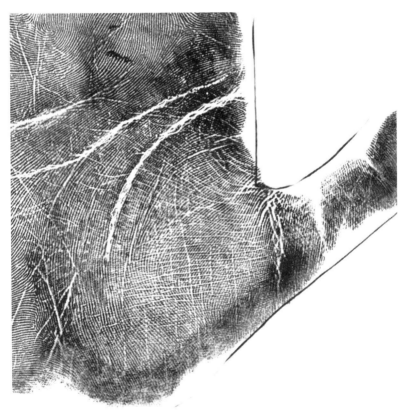

Short Vitality Line

Short lines may have plenty of energy in the short term, but can't keep going for the long haul.

If the line is of poor quality (no matter how long) it will be thin and stringy with breaks and islands.

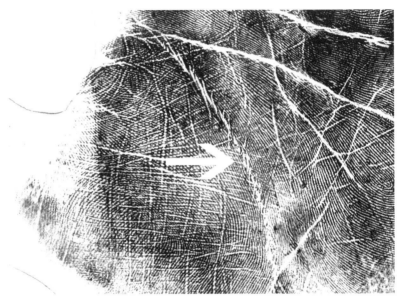

Weak Vitality Line

Usually when the Vitality Line is weak, the thumb ball is flabby or flat and the person tends to be a bit of a cold fish. This won't affect the length of their life though, and they may well go on whining about their chilblains into their nineties. A weak Vitality Line lacks vitality and they'll suffer minor illnesses more often. It's harder for a weak-rooted person to support themselves. They tend to be less able to stick at long-term commitments and are more easily overwhelmed by life's demands. A weak Vitality Line on the *passive* hand shows an insecure upbringing, where parental divorce, constant struggle, or instability was the norm.

A Vitality Line made up of islands or a series of tiny lines shows an immature, restless person with poor concentration. Usually their assimilation of food is poor and they're constantly trying new diets, lifestyles and regimes.

Nothing strengthens a Vitality Line more than establishing fixed patterns of eating, sleeping and exercising and sticking to them. Always advise this to people with a short or weak Vitality Line.

Deep roots, strong roots If the Vitality Line is long and strong, a person tends to be a stable, well-rooted soul with a sense of fam-

ily and an instinct for homemaking. Physically, they have the stamina to see things through. A strong Vitality Line psychologically, gives a sense of being 'real'; someone with their feet planted firmly on the ground.

Boxer Muhammad Ali's palms – note the strong Vitality Lines

Look at these two palm prints. One belongs to a childless,

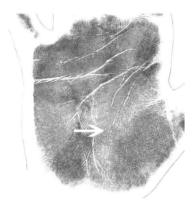

Naomi's and Amber's palms

part time sales assistant, Amber, who's moved home fourteen times in five years. She hates cooking, comes from an unstable background and finds it hard to stick at things. Her hobbies are Wicca studies and traveling.

The other line belongs to Naomi, who has three children. She's a sales assistant in the same shop as Amber. She lives close to her parents, loves to cook and to garden and hasn't moved home in ten years. Which is Naomi's palm and which is Amber's?

Hopefully it's obvious that Naomi's palm is on the left and Amber's on the right.

Wandering roots

The very bottom end of the line (near the wrist) is where our instinctive roots plant us in life. If this base segment has a fork

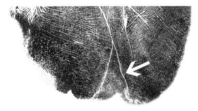

branching away from the thumb, it's like a shoot looking for new pastures. This is called a travel line and shows a need for travel and variety.

Travel line on an airline pilot's palm

This line is always split at the bottom when someone belongs to two cultures as in, for instance, second generation immigrants.

The opposite pattern, where the bottom of the line curls deep into the thumb ball, shows a

Vitality Line curling into the base of the thumb ball

person very much bound to their home and country, who

dislikes traveling.

Breaking up is hard to do

Breaks in the Vitality Line show interruptions in energy, and important shifts in one's lifestyle, rather like a plant being uprooted and replanted. This is always traumatic if there's a clear break with no overlap.

However, it can be positive if the line overlaps and is stronger after the break than before it. An improved situation and a fresh start is guaranteed in such cases.

Break and gap in the Vitality Line. This person was unable to walk for two years

The main reasons for breaks in the Vitality Line on the passive hand are the loss of a parent or sibling, parental divorce or major change in family circumstances. If the line is broken on the passive but not on the active hand, the person will create a more stable lifestyle for themselves as they get older (though there will be an

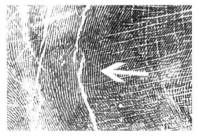

underlying sense of insecurity).

On the active hand a break shows a major life change undergone by the individual such as divorce, illness, moving house or country.

Break with overlap. This person divorced and remarried into much happier circumstances

Breaks and markings can be timed chronologically. The Vitality Line can be marked into ten-year sections and a rough

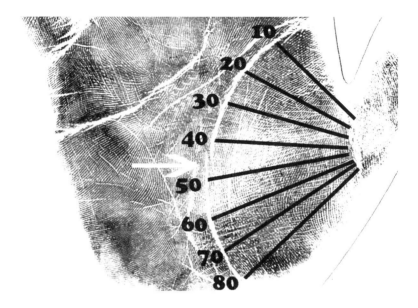

Timing on the Vitality Line. The break shows when that this person emigrated at the age of 44

idea of when an interruption occurs can be gauged.

Don't fall into the trap of making predictions based on markings on the Vitality Line. This can be negative and destructive. We are the authors of our fates. If we make changes to ourselves, we create different futures. If you see someone with breaks on their Vitality Line, don't warn them darkly of terrors ahead. Instead urge them to develop stable, healthy patterns of diet, sleep and exercise. This will improve their Vitality Line, often repairing the line and future situation.

Branches

Lines branching up off the Vitality Line are like new shoots sprouting off the root line into new uplifting experiences. They

Bar line crossing the Vitality Line. The illness of a business partner caused a period of great strain

indicate beneficial events; almost always this is an inheritance, a new job, a new child or the seizing of an opportunity.

Islands on this line show periods of stress and indecision. This is common when there are domestic and family issues.

Bar lines on the Vitality Line show exterior events interrupting one's progress in life.

Double trouble

Occasionally there are two Vitality Lines. If there are two on the passive palm it means a person had two very different parents and two senses of home.

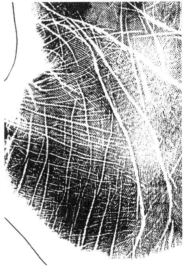

On the active hand, a person with two Vitality Lines has a lot of energy and is in constant motion. They will travel extensively; they'll have two homes, belong to two families or countries and two **Doubled Vitality Lines** distinct lifestyles.

Secret palmist assignment

Examine your Vitality Line on your active hand and see if you can time any markings or interruptions along it. Try to make connections between the major things that have happened to you, like divorce, illness, and house moves, and the markings. Ask the people whose palm prints you have, for a very brief biography with their major life changes and dates. Check them against the markings on their Vitality Lines.

Brain bashing quiz
Time given: ten minutes

1. What does it mean if a person has a short Vitality Line – will they die young?
2. What does a fork branching away from the bottom of the Vitality Line mean?
3. Would a person with a short, weak Vitality Line on their passive hand come from a stable, secure family?
4. If someone moves house a lot and are fascinated by angels and spirits, what kind of Vitality Line would they have?
5. What's the difference between a clean break and an overlap on the Vitality Line?
6. Does a doubled Vitality Line make one schizophrenic?
7. If there are small lines rising up off the Vitality Line do they show illnesses?
8. Should you predict danger ahead from a negative marking on the Vitality Line?
9. Roughly what age is a point half way down the Vitality Line?

Answers are on the next page

HOUR FIFTEEN
LIGHT OF THE MIND – THE
LINE OF CONSCIOUSNESS

Mental illumination

The Line of Consciousness (traditionally called the 'head line') is an important indicator of character. It shows the way we think and this is a vital aspect of our personality. Whether or not someone is philosophical, practical, level-headed, surreal, focused or easily distracted is easily observed from the Line of Consciousness.

A good metaphor for this line is a beam of light. The clarity of thought, our ability to mentally 'see', is dependant on the length, boldness and straightness of this light beam.

If this line is the *strongest* one on the palm, a person's energy is burned up in thinking, planning and speculating. They may well be intelligent, but they won't have any energy for the basics of life, like exercising, cooking, shopping and raising children. They'll

Answers

1. No. A short Vitality Line means they lack vitality, are ungrounded and insecure and find it difficult to support themselves.
2. A branch at the bottom of this line gives an inclination for travel, change and new experiences.
3. No. Their background would have been unstable and insecure.
4. A short or weak one.
5. A clean break shows a difficult, vulnerable time without stability for the length of the gap, an overlap shows a difficult time but a move into new experiences.
6. On the passive palm two lines means very different parents and two senses of home. On the active it gives abundant energy with two homes, families or countries to belong to and two distinct lifestyles.
7. No. Rising branches show aspirations and new, positive experiences.
8. No. Simply advise a stable, healthy lifestyle.
9. A point half-way down the line is about 43 years of age

have difficulty sleeping whenever there's something on their minds.

Searchlight minds

The longer this line, the more a person mentally thinks ahead, and the more they consider when making a decision. A person with a long line ending under the antenna digit thinks a long way into the future, and they'll consider lots of possibilities before deciding anything. Long lines like to instruct, learn and ponder. They're often 'Know-alls'; strong characters with lots to say who know a little about a lot. They tend to enjoy quizzes and mind puzzles – they like obscure facts and abstract knowledge and spend a long time processing information. A long line will philosophize over the implications of events. As a general rule, people with long lines tend to read much more than people with short lines.

A long Line of Consciousness on the palm of a researcher

Often people with very long lines of consciousness are eccentric mavericks that 'think outside the box'. Mental brilliance though is as much about the *clarity* of the line as the length. The most sharp, intellectual, focused and mentally proficient minds have a long Line of Consciousness that's fine and clear, like a laser beam.

Going all the way

If the Line of Consciousness crosses the palm *completely from side-to-side* this creates a person that can be ruthlessly unsentimental and one that has an obsessive mentality. They can't stop thinking and they easily cut themselves off from their feelings.

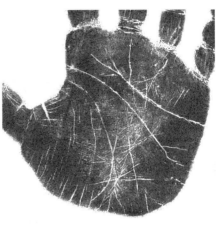

Einstein's Line of Consciousness

Completely crossing Line of Consciousness

Table-lamp minds

A short line (ending under the wall finger area) indicates someone who lives in the now and who considers only their immediate circumstances. These lines are found on people who get stuck into life and who don't analyze too much. They tend to develop one particular specialist skill and focus on one particular area of life. They apply their knowledge practically. It's like their light beam brings their immediate surroundings into sharp focus. People with short Line of Consciousness don't think things through to their conclusion and don't see the long-term implications of their actions. They're materialistic and they don't want to study subjects that aren't related to the 'real' world. They're 'doers' and often highly skilled people, who don't waste time staring into the future.

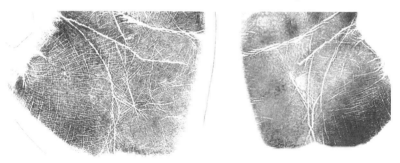

One of these hands is that of a financial consultant, specializing in long-term investments, the other is a plumber. Which is which?

Hopefully, it's obvious the consultant's palm is on the left

Fuzzy minded

If the Line of Consciousness is broken up, or full of little islands and crossing lines, no matter how long the line, a person will have poor mental focus.

They simply can't think clearly. Their mental light-beam is

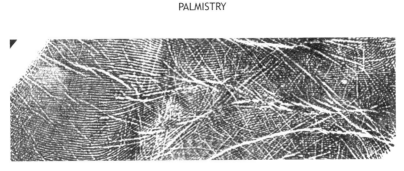

Weak, broken Line of Consciousness

fuzzy. This is a sign of someone who'll have trouble asserting themselves.

On the level or round the bend?

You could say the world is split into people with straight lines of consciousness and those with bent ones. The two types see the world in different terms.

Straight

Straight Line of Consciousness people think straight, they're to the point; their thinking is logical and rational. Long straight lines are great ones for 'isms, – socialism, atheism, vegetarianism. They like structured, logical systems of thinking. Blunt, and unsentimental, they love facts.

A straight line avoids dipping into the Sea of Subconscious area of the palm (remember covering the areas of the palm in Chapter Eleven?). This makes them unwilling to be

A straight Line of Consciousness

sentimental or to delve into their own pasts, dreams or deeper selves. They love sunshine and strong light and like ideas that are clear, bright and obvious. They are mistrustful of obscure, cryptic and illogical ideas. An art house movie or a cryptic crossword would leave them baffled.

Bent

People with bent or sloping Lines of Consciousness understand that everything is a matter of perspective. Their view of reality is 'bent' and not straightforward. These people are 'deep', their Line of Consciousness dips into the Sea of Subconscious area, so

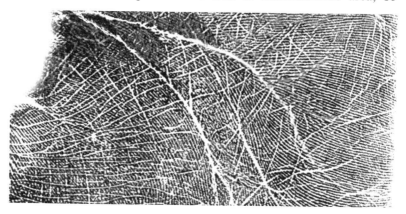

Bent Line of Consciousness

they're often lost in their deeper selves.

They see the world subjectively and can get things out of proportion. These people aren't level-headed, their world view changes as their moods change. They love the artistic and the mystical. They like darkness and shadows, moonlight and candles; they need to shut themselves off from the world to spend time alone. They love psychoanalysis, dreams, the arts and anything that allows them to delve into themselves. They can make connections that are neither linear nor logical and this can be highly imaginative. Artists, introverts, poets, spiritual aspirants and loners tend to have bent lines. They internalize things and often need art to express themselves as words are inadequate. People with very bent Lines of Consciousness often work alone or in small groups of people where they can burrow away and where they don't have to respond quickly to an ever-ringing phone, or meet urgent targets. They can be intensely moody.

Beginnings

The beginning of the Line of Consciousness is a measure of how open and adventurous a person is. The greater the distance between the Vitality Line and the Line of Consciousness, the more confident and independent their mental vision. The more the line clings to the Vitality Line the more a person mentally clings to what they know. Some stand on a stepladder to see to the far horizon, while some are pressed to the earth and see a snail's-eye view. Check out Einstein's air line to see a large gap between these two lines.

If the gap here is very wide on both hands, say a centimeter or more, a person will have confidence in their own views which are independent (and usually at odds with) those of their family. Such individuals tend to live a long way from their roots and are very open minded. They tend to be ambitious, and live on a higher cultural plane than their parents, seeking out exotic ideas and experiences.

Where the Line of Consciousness is tied to the Vitality Line so the two are joined together for a centimeter or two, it's often the sign of dominating parents.

Tied lines of Vitality and Consciousness

Such a sign gives little confidence in one's own opinions. People with tied Lines of Consciousness often live close to their roots and rarely move out of their depth in life. It's common on members of ultra-orthodox religious groups who lack the capacity for independent thought.

Usually the gap is much smaller on the passive hand, showing that confidence and independence of thought grows as one matures. But it can be the other way around, where a person may be rebellious when young but becomes more conservative with maturity.

A tied Line of Consciousness on Osama Bin Laden's palm

Forks

Whenever you see a big fork at the end of the Line of Consciousness you have a mind that is diverse and able to express two different aspects of personality. An individual may have, for instance, both a straight section and a bent branch coming off it. This means they'll need to be both practical and outward-going and dreamy and introverted. An example might be,

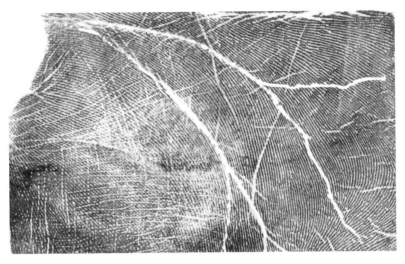

Forked Line of Consciousness

say, an estate agent who practices meditation or a mechanic who is also a poet.

A small fork at the end of the line gives a good use of language - it's often known as a 'writer's fork'. A small rising line at the end of the line going upward towards the antenna digit makes one a shrewd master of business and of money-making schemes.

Breaks

A break in the line shows a time when mentally, one doesn't function. This is usually a trauma or breakdown. If the line suddenly changes direction or renews itself after a break, the personality undergoes a dramatic change.

Islands

Islands on the Line of Consciousness always indicate a stressful state of mind. Where there's an island, the mind distorts things out of proportion.

Always advise a stress-reduction program to those with an island on this line.

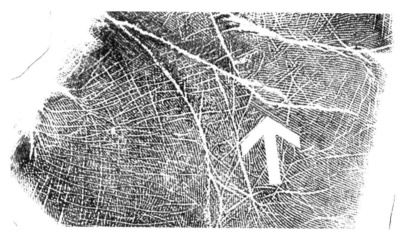

An island on the Line of Consciousness

Doubled lines

A doubled Line of Consciousness is very rare, but shows a doubling of the personality, someone that operates as a different person in two spheres of life. Usually the different personalities are split between professional and social lives, and often the person displays different mannerisms and speech patterns within these two spheres.

Doubled Lines of Consciousness

Secret palmist assignment

Try to guess what kind of Line of Consciousness your friends and relatives may have. If they are for instance, introverted, private and imaginative by nature they'll have a deeply curved line. If they are adventurous and open minded, they'll have a big gap between this line and the Vitality Line. When you've thought about it, try to sneak a look at their Lines of Consciousness and test out your assumptions.

What kind of Line of Consciousness do you have? This line is the quickest to change. Make sure you have a copy of your own hand prints as the line will probably lengthen and grow as you work you way through this book.

Brain bashing quiz
Time given: ten minutes

1. If a person has a short Line of Consciousness does it mean they're stupid?
2. What's the difference between a straight and a bent Line of Consciousness?
3. Would a person with a Line of Consciousness tied to the beginning of the Vitality Line have a broad, adventurous mind set?
4. What does it mean if an individual has a Line of Consciousness that crosses the palm completely, side to side?
5. If someone loves their own space, is introverted and dreamy and loves the arts, what kind of a Line of Consciousness

would they have?

6. If someone were muddle-headed, timid and easily led, what kind of Line of Consciousness would they have?

7. What does it mean if the Line of Consciousness is clear and fine, like a laser beam?

8. What does it mean to have an island on the Line of Consciousness?

9. Does a big fork at the end of this line make a person a genius?

Answers are on the next page.

HOUR SIXTEEN
RIVER OF FEELING – THE LINE OF EMOTION

Cry me a river...

The Line of Emotion is about how we experience our feelings. It's like a river that floods us with impressions of the exterior world. The deeper and longer the line, the more emotionally responsive we are. This line isn't simply about relationships, but how we react emotively to a song, a whiff of perfume or a weepy movie.

Strength

If the Line of Emotion is the most strongly marked one on the palm, a person would be ruled by their feelings. Their energy would come and go as their feelings changed.

A deep red Line of Emotion shows deeply felt emotions. A weak, faint line shows weakly experienced feelings.

When the line is faint and broken up, with lots of islands and

---

Answers

1. No. A short line means they're focused on the here and now and are likely to develop practical skills.
2. A straight-lined person thinks logically and rationally. They're level-headed. A bent-lined person is subjective, they make connections that are not linear and this can be creative, relative and highly imaginative.
3. No. They'd be narrow-minded and unsure of their own ideas.
4. Side to side lines create an obsessive-minded person who can't stop thinking.
5. They'd have a bent Line of Consciousness that moved deep into the Sea of Subconscious area.
6. A fuzzy, weak, broken-up Line of Consciousness.
7. A fine, clear line shows an acute, highly perceptive, sharp mind.
8. Islands show a stressful mind-set.
9. No. A large fork indicates a versatile personality that needs to be both practical and artistic.

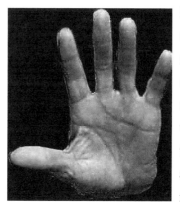

A dominant Line of Emotion on Michael Jackson's palm

interruptions, a person is confused about their feelings. They tend to be moody, unstable and emotionally complex. They aren't clear what song their heart is singing. People with weak lines of emotion tend to drink a lot of fluids: tea, coffee and alcohol. They're unable to relax easily and to experience rich, spontaneous emotions.

It's common to see lines of emotion broken and corrupted, probably as a result of a society based on rational, factual and analytical structures. We may mourn the loss of the heart's reign over the human condition, but it must be remembered that if our passions ruled our minds, we'd be back in the dark ages very quickly. A poor quality Line of Emotion can be quickly improved by learning to trust instinctive emotions, through, for instance, free-form dancing or singing.

Length

The line always starts at the edge of the palm under the antenna

An ideal Line of Emotion

finger, but varies greatly in where it ends. The ideal, balanced ending would be for it to curve up between the mirror and wall digits.

If the line's short, ending somewhere under the wall

A short Line of Emotion

finger, a person would be limited in their emotional responses, especially if the line is also weak. They'd be unromantic and rather cool emotionally. They may be responsive to their family, pet dog or football team, but their friendships would be extremely limited and businesslike. This is often found on socially isolated people.

The longer the line, the more people one responds to. If the line is very long, crossing the palm completely from palm edge to palm edge, an individual would have a compulsion to respond to others.

This is often found on generously-spirited doctors, care workers and therapists. Ironically, this

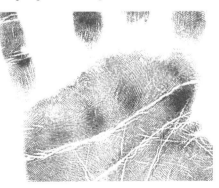

A Line of Emotion that completely crosses the palm

pattern means they repress their own personal emotional needs.

People with short Lines of Emotion are less enduring than those with long ones – they might be your best friend one moment and forget your existence the next. A long line holds on to relationships for a long time and makes a lot of connections to a lot of people. Their address books are always full.

Curving upward

An upward curvature of the line indicates an idealistic feeling response and shows one is strongly expressive of one's masculinity or femininity. On the passive hand, a strong upward curve to this line shows the parents demonstrated strongly conventional sexual roles. Lines that curve upwards are passionate, romantic and expressive, clear about their gender role.

Beautiful dreamer

If the Line of Emotion runs up into the mirror digit, this makes for an emotional idealist. The bearer of this sign will possess a wonderful optimism, is likely to over-romanticize life and is often

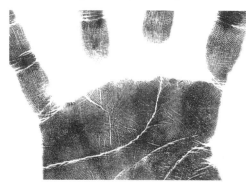

A Line of Emotion going to the wall finger

spiritually inclined. However, they are unrealistic about their emotional expectations and can be sadly disappointed.

The pragmatist

If the line curves up into the wall finger,

common sense and practicality rules the emotions. These people want a steady, reliable partner and financial security.

These aren't romantically adventurous folk, though they are faithful and dutiful.

Curving downward

If the line bends downward, it represents an unwillingness to express a traditional sense of one's sexuality.

So a man with this marking may hate football, have long hair and display a distinct feminine side, while a woman with the same marking would never wear a skirt or make-up, for example. **A downward curving line**

The green-eyed monster

Jealousy on the palm is easily seen by a branch or ending of the Line of Emotion that runs downward towards or touches the Vitality Line. These 'jealousy lines' show emotional insecurity and a need for lots of reassurance. If this sign is on the *passive*

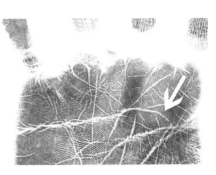

A 'jealousy' line dropping towards the Vitality Line

hand, it can indicate 'hands off' parenting without much physical affection, or someone that can't let go of their parents.

If the dropping line is the *only* ending this could cause problems in relationships. People with this formation are also excessively sentimental about the past and can't let go.

Straight

Straight lines of emotion are less sure of what the goal of their affections is.

A straight Line of Emotion

They're unsubtle and unromantic; a whimsical poem wouldn't work for them. They like emotional signals that are clear and direct. They're generally unsure of who the 'right one' is. If the line is deep and red, they can be direct, sexually.

Broken lines, broken hearts

If the Line of Emotion has a break in it, this shows a break in an individual's ability to feel for a period of time (there's an example of this in Chapter Thirteen).

It's always a response to some serious emotional loss or disappointment, like divorce or death of a loved one.

A second, 'broken-off', higher section of the line

It's particularly common to see the end section of the line broken off. When you see a break and a new section of the line beginning a lot higher up the palm, it shows someone that operates on two emotional levels.

They have a public 'front' where they're lively and apparently emotionally expressive, but have a deeper level of more ambiguous responses privately. They often experience confusion about what they're really feeling. If this sign is on the *passive* hand, it's a response to the experience of some sense of emotional disappointment, like the divorce of parents. Advise time alone for people with this sign, they often try too hard when in the presence of others.

Islands and branches

An island on this line shows a period of emotional confusion. A branch shooting upwards show an emotive high and dropping lines show emotional losses.

The tangled knots we weave...

Don't be surprised to find Lines of Emotion with two or three different endings. There may be, for instance, a line going to the mirror finger, a 'jealousy line' dropping to the Vitality Line and a branch of the line reaching up to the wall finger. In this case, a person would be a romantic idealist, but would have a need to make practical emotional judgments and would also suffer jealousy and insecurity. Our emotional realms are often the most complex of our drives and this is where a palmist is invaluable. Explaining these complicated and opposing needs can help a person enormously.

The flirt

A common sign is a sort of spray of small lines at the end of

Flirtation lines

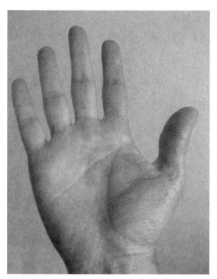

Simian line on ex UK Prime Minister Tony Blair's palm

the Line of Emotion. This indicates a flirt, someone that needs to connect to lots of people on lots of different levels. Usually they have very diverse friendships.

One-liners

Occasionally (in around one person in a hundred) the Line of Emotion and the Line of Consciousness fuse together to create a single line. This is called a simian line.

This is the sign of an obsessive and highly repressive personality. Thought and feeling mix together, so they do what they do with all of their being to the exclusion of everything else. They always tend to be remarkable in some way, if only for their relentless, one-track personalities. It's extremely difficult for a simian-lined person to be 'rational'; they're permanently in an excited state, rather as an average person is when angry or worked up.

Simian-lined folk have tunnel vision and find it difficult to see things from another's point of view. This sign is often found on great achievers. Because they are so repressed and because they take things to extremes, they find change difficult. Always advise a simian-lined person to find some form of relaxation to give them a sense of peace.

Secret palmist assignment

Try to get a glimpse of the Line of Emotion on your friends and relatives. Because we tend to hide our emotional selves, you'll probably be surprised at what kind of lines they have. See if you can check the palm of a professional nurse, therapist or care worker – you'll find their Line of Emotion is particularly long or strong.

What kind of Line of Emotion do you have? Is it the strongest line on your palm, so you're dominated by your feelings? Are you an idealist? Are you passionate, jealous, or somewhat 'cool'?

Brain bashing quiz
Time given: ten minutes

1. If a person has a short Line of Emotion does it mean they're romantic?
2. What's the difference between a straight and an upwardly bent Line of Emotion?
3. Would a person with a Line of Emotion that crossed the palm side-to-side be expressive emotionally?
4. What does it mean if an individual has a Line of Emotion that

curves up to the wall digit?

5. If someone were possessive and jealous, what sort of line formation would indicate this?

6. What does it mean if the Line of Emotion is weak and broken up?

7. What does it mean to have a 'spray' of little lines at the end of the Line of Emotion?

8. Is a siman-lined person relaxed and open hearted?

9. If there are three different endings to the Line of Emotion does it mean a person is a sociopath?

Answers are on the next page.

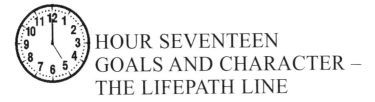

HOUR SEVENTEEN
GOALS AND CHARACTER –
THE LIFEPATH LINE

Strength of character

The Lifepath Line (traditionally called the fate line) is the most difficult major line to locate on the palm. It's often weak, or it's only partially present. It begins near the base of the palm and wanders upward, toward the wall digit. Occasionally, it's absent altogether. Unlike the other major lines, this one often doesn't develop until after the age of twenty or so when we 'find ourselves' and our sense of purpose.

When you see a clear, bold Lifepath Line, it means a person has established a clear sense of their own character; they have goals and values of their own.

This line is strongly associated with the career, as this is a vital

---

Answers

1. No. They'd have a limited range of emotions. This is often found on socially isolated people.
2. Straight lines of emotion are unsubtle and unromantic. Upward curved lines are passionate, romantic and expressive.
3. No. This would make a person obsessed with caring for others, but personally repressed, emotionally.
4. This gives common-sense emotions. A drive for a steady, reliable partner and financial security.
5. A Line of Emotion that drops down to the Vitality Line or a branch of the line that does the same thing.
6. This indicates complicated emotional patterns. A broken-up line means a person will be emotionally complex and unstable.
7. This is the sign of a flirt.
8. No. They are fixated, intense and obsessive.
9. No. This is common and shows a complex set of emotional ideals.

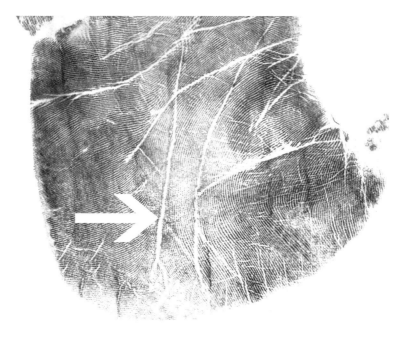

A clear Lifepath Line

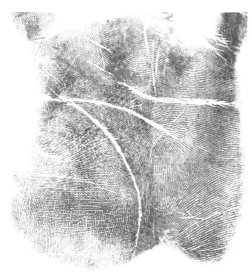

Missing Lifepath Line

aspect of our lifepath. When there isn't a Lifepath Line visible in someone's palm, a person never knows what it is they want to be or do.

They have the freedom to do anything, but tend to feel unbalanced and unfulfilled. People tend to be much more content when they have a clear Lifepath Line than when they don't.

If the Lifepath Line is the *strongest* line on the palm, it makes for a strong character, uncompromising about who they are and what they want. They tend to be difficult, defensive people with a sense of society being against them.

Remember that not having this line doesn't mean one doesn't have a job, it only means you haven't defined *your own sense* of what you want out of life. A clear Lifepath Line doesn't necessarily mean one has a brilliant career, only that a person works on their own terms in their own way towards what they want out of life.

Over-strong Lifepath Line on ex Palestinian leader Yasser Arafat's palm

A window cleaner who's self-employed will have a stronger Lifepath Line than a bank manager whose life is ruled by a corporation.

Scratching a living?

You often see a faint, scratchy, poorly formed Lifepath Line on people with brilliant careers, like lawyers, show-biz people, estate agents and advertising executives.

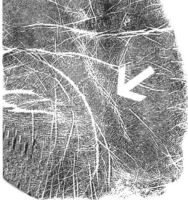

This is because they have a faint, poorly-formed character,

This weak Lifepath Line is on the palm of a barrister

and they are burning themselves out, trying to be what society wants them to be.

Begin at the beginning

The most important part of the line is the point where it starts. The Lifepath Line can start joined to the Vitality Line, or from the centre of the palm or from within the Sea of Subconscious.

When it starts joined to the Vitality Line a person has based their character and goals on their roots, parents and background.

They'll follow the family profession or parent-directed choice of work and their career will be traditional, structured and conventional.

Work is all about providing money and security. People with this marking refer to their family constantly; their whole personality is based on their family.

The Lifepath Line of a claims adjuster in the family insurance company

If the line starts in the Sea of Subconscious it shows the career and life goals are based on a person's need for personal satisfaction. This pattern means a person has followed a course in life

Lifepath Line from Sea of Subconscious in Leonardo Di Caprio's palm – note also the long peacock digit

opposite to what their background dictated and what their parents would have wanted.

A line from this area is always about working with people and using social skills. Anyone who works with the public has this sign and anyone with a career based on their creativity.

When the line starts low down in the centre of the palm, as in the first picture of this chapter, this shows a well balanced person who developed an early sense of maturity.

Late developers

Often this line doesn't develop until later in life; it's common to find it starting half-way up the palm. This always coincides with a person 'finding themselves' mid-life, a time when they experience a sense of balance and become much clearer about who they are and what they want to do. Timing is marked on this line from the bottom to the top. The point where it crosses the Line of Consciousness coincides with the age of 35 – 40. Where it crosses the Line of Emotion coincides with age 55-60.

Whenever you find the Lifepath Line missing, it's important to advise a person to get to know themselves better. Only through self-knowledge can we start to move towards what we really want out of life.

Going all the way

Do you remember learning that a line crossing the palm makes an obsessive? Well, if the Lifepath Line goes all the way to the top of the palm, a person will feel stuck in their work and lifepath and be obsessed with their duties and responsibilities. They are quick to devote their whole lives to one particular path and often feel this is their destiny. They often sense that fate moves them in life. They are drawn to religious or spiritual paths. They need to be advised to loosen up and let go of the past and to have life-changing experiences.

Joining lines

Where you see a new line from the Sea of Subconscious area *joining* or *replacing* an existing Lifepath Line, it indicates a change of direction in life. At the chronological point where the new line

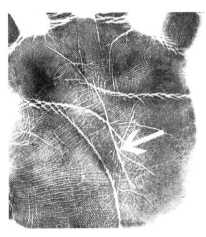

starts, there's a greater emphasis on a person's own needs and work-choice becomes based on personal satisfaction rather than material security.

Life-changing new relationships are also indicated by this marking.

This new line joining an existing one marks a time when this person changed career from receptionist to massage therapist

Castaways

Islands in the Lifepath Line indicate periods of unemployment, confusion about who one is and a sense of being lost in life. Short crossing lines indicate crisis points where we have to make life-changing decisions.

It's interesting to note that the Lifepath Line is becoming weaker on the palms of people in Western societies. This is because there are so many pressures and distractions that weaken our sense of identity. It's becoming harder and harder to know who we are. For those with no Lifepath Line, a palm reading is a vital step in getting to know themselves better. Any practice which increases self-knowledge should be encouraged.

Secret palmist assignment

Examine the Lifepath Lines on the palms of ten people. Compare the lines of strong characters who don't care about status and those who strive at prestige jobs with high salaries. You'll find the weaker Lifepath Lines are on the high-status job people. Those who don't know what they want out of life won't have a Lifepath Line at all.

Brain bashing quiz
Time given: ten minutes

1. What does it mean if a person's Lifepath Line starts half-way up their palm?
2. What's the difference between a Lifepath Line that begins in the Sea of Subconscious and one that begins tied to the Vitality Line?
3. If a person's Lifepath Line is the strongest one on their palm, does it mean they're a millionaire?
4. What does it mean if the Lifepath Line begins low down, in the centre of the palm?
5. What does it mean if the Lifepath Line is thin and scratchy?
6. What does an island on the Lifepath Line mean?

7. Is the Lifepath Line getting stronger in modern times?

8. When this line crosses the Line of Consciousness, does it coincide with age 25?

9. If the Lifepath Line is missing, should you advise a person to take any job that's going?

Answers are on the next page.

HOUR EIGHTEEN
MAJOR TO MINOR –
THE MINOR LINES

Expect the unexpected

Unlike major lines, which are almost always present in one form or another, the minor lines may well be missing. Any and every minor line may or may not be present on anyone's palm.

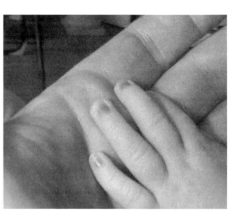

The minor lines tend to be much fainter and finer than the major lines. They change much more quickly, too, often in just a

Answers

1. This is a point mid-life when a person 'finds themselves', becoming much clearer about who they are and what they want to do.
2. If the Lifepath Line begins tied to the Vitality Line, it means a person bases their personal choices on their roots, parents and family tradition. If it begins in the Sea of Subconscious, life choices are based on personal satisfaction, social connections and creativity.
3. No. It means a strong character, uncompromising about who they are and what they want.
4. This indicates a well balanced person who developed an early sense of maturity.
5. A weak line shows a person with a poor sense of themselves, who's striving to achieve the popular ideal of success.
6. Islands indicate a time when one may be unemployed, confused about who one is and somewhat lost in life.
7. No. The Lifepath Line is becoming progressively weaker.
8. No. This point coincides with ages 35-40.
9. No. They need to get to know themselves better before establishing a career.

week or so.

Very occasionally, you'll find a minor line that's *stronger* than all the other lines on the palm, including the major lines. This isn't a good sign. It means a person's ability to function is undermined by some fixation or hurt. It's often the sign of psychological or physical disturbance.

We'll cover the minor lines from the top of the palm, working down toward the base. Take your time over these; you need to be sure you know what each line means and how to recognize it. When you examine a palm, if there's only a barely visible, scratchy remnant of a minor line visible, ignore it.

Fantasy line (Ring of Saturn, Girdle of Venus)

This is a fine horizontal line (or more often, a series of short horizontal lines) above the Line of Emotion. Don't confuse this with a broken-off section of the Line of Emotion.

This line gives a need to escape into higher realms and a

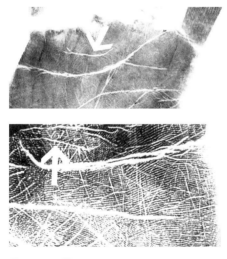

Fantasy lines

frustration with concrete reality. A person with this marking is sensitive and idealistic with a particular drive to get 'out of their heads'. Negatively, this might mean through alcohol or taking drugs, or in being so idealistic and dreamy they don't engage with life. Positively, this line gives a tremendous capacity to the imagination and can make for an inspired artist, web designer or a person devoted to a spiritual path. This line's usually seen on those that seek a new form of reality, be it a spiritual, cultural, virtual or visionary. They're always drawn to unusual lifestyles and will seek a strong partner, more earth-bound than themselves, as a sort of anchor.

Affection lines

The affection lines are on the outer edge of the palm beneath the antenna finger. You'll need to twist the palm, edge-on to see them properly. Traditional palmists associated these lines with the number of marriages and children a person will have, which is ridiculous.

The average person has one to three of these lines, each around a centimeter long. Where, as in the majority of us, this is the case, ignore these lines completely.

Sometimes the line is longer than average, extending for a couple of centimeters parallel to and above the Line of Emotion. This gives a strong emotional ideal of the perfect partner. Though the search may take years, when the match is at last made (maybe

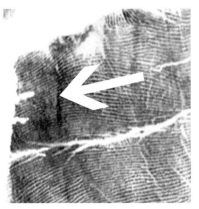
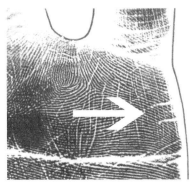

Typical affection lines

a marriage or two down the road) the person makes a tremendous, romantic love bond that won't be broken.

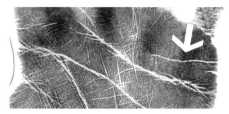

An extra-long affection line

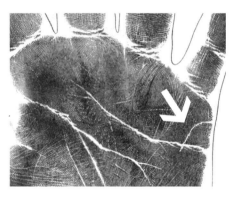

A plunging affection line – this is a two-time divorcée

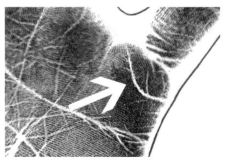

An affection line cutting off the antenna finger

If the affection line runs all the way down to touch or cross the Line of Emotion this is called a 'divorce line'. It indicates an impulse to connect with the 'wrong' partner.

Invariably, adults of middle age with this sign have experienced at least one divorce or serious separation. These patterns need to be explained to anyone with this marking to help them make the right choices in relationships.

If the line runs *upward* to cut off the antenna finger, it cuts off the digit of sexuality.

Usually, it's a sign of inhibition about sexual experiences or fear of intimacy. Often people with this sign stay outside sexual relationships for long periods of time.

Passion line

This one always gets people excited, desperately scouring their own and their friend's hands for any indication of this line!

The passion line is a straight, angular line that runs from the centre of the Line of Emotion and moves up towards the little finger.

It gives an elevated sexual imagination and a highly visual side to sexuality. The bearers of this line always need to find a partner physically attractive.

It's found on anyone that enjoys literary and visual erotica and one that enjoys role playing, risqué and voyeuristic aspects of sexual behavior. It's only found on around ten per cent of the general population, but is found in much higher proportion in those that are into partner-swapping, pornography, escapist sexual fantasy and the more racy aspects of sexuality.

Bear in mind that this line doesn't give you a strong sex *drive* – this is more a question of the size of the thumb ball and the strength of the Vitality Line. This line is only about the sexual *imagination*. Anyone with this line has a vivid erotic fantasy world. It doesn't necessarily mean a person will have a colorful love life; they may prefer their sexual fantasies to remain as just that.

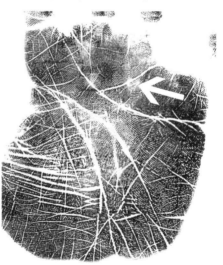

Passion line

Peace and privacy – the Inner Realm line (Apollo line, Line of Sun)

This line is extremely fine and runs vertically below the peacock finger. Nearly everyone has a section of this line above the Line of Emotion, but that's of no consequence.

Typical Inner Realm line

It's when the line is present further down, *below* the Line of Emotion that it's worthy of mention.

If there's a clear, fine, straight line, more than two centimeters long, it shows a kind of inner contentment. People with this line have developed an ability to withdraw from life into their own inner space. It shows a drive to seek peace and quiet and to love one's personal privacy. This marking is always a sign that someone spends a lot of time contentedly alone.

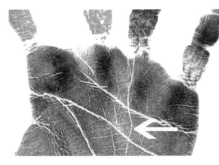

Inner Realm line on the palm of a Tai-chi master

The line is developed when people can become completely absorbed and 'forget themselves' in an activity. This is usually in some meditative process, in, for instance, spiritual healing or Tai chi or when practicing art or therapy.

However, it's also found on those that 'tune out' of the world in more mundane ways, in, say, gardening, or walking the dog. It's an important marker on the road of spiritual development.

Nervous Activity line (Hepatica, Mercury line)

This line is usually in the form of a single line or a fine series of vertical lines half-way down the palm in the Sea of Subconscious area, just underneath or crossing the end of the Line of Consciousness. The Nervous Activity Line shows activity of the parasympathetic nervous system which governs the digestion, breathing and other automatic physical processes. If there's a series of broken lines or a very deep, trench-like line, an overactive nervous system is negatively affecting the digestion and health generally.

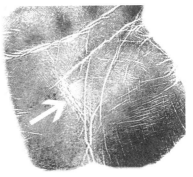

Poor-quality Nervous Activity line

The elderly are much more likely to display a too deep or broken line formation than the young. It's often later in life when we suffer from 'nerves' and digestion becomes more fragile as a result.

It's a sign of mental brilliance, however, if the line is clear, fine and straight.

In this form it's often seen on 'ideas' people – writers, inventors, innovators and those that can snatch ideas out of the air.

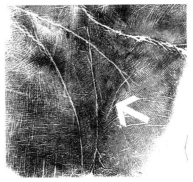

Clear Nervous Activity line on the palm of a writer

Spirit line

This is easily confused with the Nervous Activity line as it's found in the same place. It's curved, rather than straight however, and needs to run all the way from the base of the Sea of Subconscious up to the Line of Emotion to be a good example. It's a very rare sign and shows psychic gifts.

A Spirit Line on the hand of a Medium

Often people with this line are terrified of psychic phenomena as they're so open and receptive to such experiences.

Battle line (Mars line)

This line is usually present in some broken, scratchy form in most people's palms.

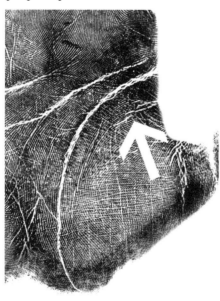

It's found within the web of skin just below the top section of the Vitality Line. Only when you see a clear, unbroken example at least two centimeters in length should you take it into account. It gives extra energy and passion, a drive to push oneself and tendency to admire courageous exploits. Individuals with a clear Battle line usually enjoy sports and challenges.

Typical Battle line

Secret palmist assignment

When looking for minor lines you need to examine the palm extra carefully, so you'd best work from a print. This means you can work without pressure. Take the prints of ten people and look for their minor lines – it may help to use a magnifying glass. When you find a clear example of any minor line, make a note of it. Talk to your sample people about the characteristics shown by their minor line markings. Don't be too surprised if they seem a little shocked that you could know so much!

Clear Battle line on the palm of a martial artist

Brain bashing quiz
Time given: ten minutes

1. What does it mean if a person has an affection line that plunges down to touch or cross the Line of Emotion?
2. Would you find a Fantasy line on a down-to-earth person?
3. Is a person with a Fantasy line likely to seek an artistic partner?
4. What's the difference between a clear, fine, straight Nervous Activity line and a line that's broken up?
5. If a person's has a clear Inner Realm line are they psychic?

6. Would a person with a passion line have a rich sexual imagination?

7. Does a clear Battle line make someone a student of famous battles?

8. If a person has a clear Spirit line do they have psychic ability?

9. Do you find a lot of poor quality Nervous Activity lines on the young?

Answers are on the next page.

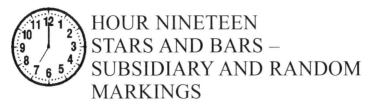

HOUR NINETEEN
STARS AND BARS –
SUBSIDIARY AND RANDOM
MARKINGS

The end is nigh

You've only got this chapter to wade through and you'll know all the signs, markings and indications on the palm. Keep going, you're almost there!

The markings we're looking at in this chapter are more obscure, less important and less likely to be present than the ones in the previous chapter. We'll go through these, starting in the Primal Home and Body quadrant (hopefully, you're familiar with the various palm areas by now, but if not, check back to Chapter Eleven). We'll work clockwise from this quadrant, around the palm.

Markings on the Primal Home and Body quadrant

Often you'll find fine lines radiating out from the thumb, running

Answers

1. This is known as a 'divorce' line, it indicates an impulse to connect with the 'wrong' partner.
2. No. Fantasy Lines are found on people that find concrete reality difficult.
3. No. People with this marking tend to seek a well grounded partner.
4. A broken up Nervous Activity line (or a deep, trench-like one) shows an over active nervous system is negatively affecting the digestion and health generally. If the line is clear, fine and straight, a person can snatch ideas out of the air.
5. Not necessarily. An inner realm line means a person can tune out of the world and become completely absorbed in an activity.
6. Yes. This may or may not be lived out in reality.
7. No. A battle line gives extra strength and passion and a drive to push oneself.
8. Yes, potentially. They may choose to ignore this ability, though.
9. No. These are much more common on the elderly when we are much more prone to nervous complaints.

Stress lines

across the Primal Home and Body quadrant to the Vitality Line. These are stress lines.

If there are only three or four fine lines, this is normal. If there are a multitude of lines, particularly if they cross the Vitality Line, it shows physical stress, a restless disposition and problems within the family or home. Usually they'll have difficulty sleeping. Often this is a sign of someone moving house.

Support lines

Lots of lines running *downward* inside and parallel to the Vitality Line are called support lines. They are rather like a sort of scaffolding that sustain us in life. These lines show that we need our friends, habits and routines to keep ourselves going.

Too many of these indicate a slightly neurotic person who takes half the house, their yoga DVDs, a diet sheet,

Support lines

vitamin tablets and all their contacts with them on holiday. They live a life with lots of props.

Loyalty line

This marking is very common. It's a thick crease or line that crosses the thumb ball.

It indicates a primal, tribal loyalty, which may be to the family, country, friends or favorite football team.

Loyalty line

Markings on the Sea of Subconscious
Intensity line

This is a fine, horizontal line running across the base of the Sea of Subconscious. It indicates restlessness and difficulty in relaxing completely. It's a sign of someone that loves risk and adventure.

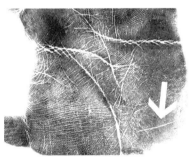

Intensity line on a mountain climber's palm

Allergy line (Via Lascivia)

This line is becoming more and more common. It's a curved line across the base of the Sea of Subconscious. It shows an over reactive and highly sensitive

Allergy line

immune system and a strong likelihood of allergies. The most common allergens are nuts, seafood, wheat and dairy products.

Markings on the World Stage quadrant

Samaritan lines (Healing Stigmata)

These are a series of very fine vertical lines, crossing the Line of Emotion under the antenna digit. They seem to excite of the Line of Emotion and suggest the need to express benevolence to others.

Samaritan lines

This sign is common on complimentary therapists, nurses, healers, and generally kind people.

Markings on the Ivory Tower quadrant

Teacher's square

This is a square made by random lines below the mirror finger and above the Line of Consciousness. This marking strengthens the sense of self in terms of organizing people. It's associated with teaching, organizing, managing others and giving instruction.

Teachers' square

Ring of Solomon

This is a very fine line that curls around the base and cuts off the self-reflective mirror finger. It gives insight into the nature of others. People with this marking are fascinated by the insightful arts – counseling, psychology, astrology and it is an excellent sign for a palmist to have. If you don't have one yet, perhaps if you stick at it you'll develop one!

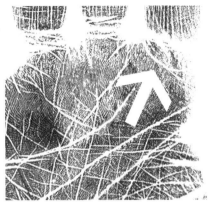

Ring of Solomon

Bars across the fingertips

You'll often see little horizontal lines on the fingertips. If there are only one or two, this is unimportant. However, if there a lots of these on *all* the fingertips, it shows extreme stress or a disturbance to the endocrinal system. It's common to see lots of these lines on women at puberty and during the menopause.

Fingertip bars. This is the palm of a man undergoing a divorce

Random markings

Every hand has a number of obscure and unique markings on its surface. There will be random crosses, circles, stars and triangles, and all manner of irregular patterns. For centuries, palmists have made much of these 'mystic crosses' and 'stars of good fortune'.

People will endlessly approach you with terror catching in their voices asking you about their 'snake' marking or their 'circle of intuition' or whatever. You are advised to forget all about such petty details. The sheer power and importance of such markings as the finger length, fingerprints, skin texture and the major lines make such indecipherable random markings pale into insignificance.

If someone has, for instance, silk skin, a long mirror finger or a whorl pattern on their thumb, these signs have a massive effect on the way they need to live and be. You now have the insight to direct, advise and guide people 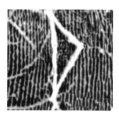 though the terrors and wonders of their journey of the soul. You are in a unique position to help people understand themselves. You can liberate them from their lifelong prisons of unknowing.

In palmistry, one should never stop learning. However long you've been practicing, you will often be puzzled by odd markings and patterns you've never seen before. Don't get hung up on them. Work always with what you do know and don't waste time on what you don't.

Secret palmist assignment

Congratulations! You've covered all the ground work and are now almost ready to launch yourself on an unsuspecting world!

Pick a person you don't know very well for your first 'blind' reading. Measure their thumb ball and skin texture and the length of their fingers and take their palm prints. Following this book, chapter by chapter, work through a complete hand reading, starting with the skin texture and ending with the subsidiary lines. Write down your findings. Compare the passive and active hands and make a note of any differences. Give all the notes you've taken to the person whose hand you've read. Listen to their feedback.

Brain bashing quiz
Time given: ten minutes

1. Do lines running inside and parallel to the Vitality Line represent the number of children you'll have?
2. Do a lot of lines crossing the Primal Home and Body area indicate countries you'll visit?
3. Where are Samaritan lines found and what do they look like?
4. Is a Teacher's square found on the mirror finger?
5. Does a cross under the wall finger mean you'll win the lottery?
6. Is a Loyalty line rare? Where is it found?
7. Do bars on the fingertips show endocrinal over-activity and/or stress?
8. What does it mean if a person has an Intensity line?
9. Would a person with an Allergy line enjoy radiant health?

Answers are on the next page.

HOUR TWENTY
LET'S PUT IT ALL TOGETHER

Almost there

If you've worked your way through all the chapters and exercises to this point, well done! You're now in possession of all the knowledge necessary to be a real palmist. All you need now is experience and a little confidence and you can fly!

The magic of hand reading begins when you put all the points you've learned together to build a complete picture of an individual.

Some general guidance

Let's go over a few pointers to get you going. Firstly, palmistry is a powerful art indeed. People have no protection, no barriers against you. By showing you their palms, a person is revealing everything. You're looking deep below the surface personality and

Answers

1. No. Lines parallel to the Vitality Line represent the people, habits and structures in one's life.
2. No. Horizontal lines on the Primal Home and Body area are stress lines relating to the home, family or lifestyle.
3. Samaritan lines are fine, vertical lines that cross the Line of Emotion under the antenna digit.
4. No. The teacher's square is found beneath the mirror digit.
5. No. Obscure crosses and random markings should be ignored.
6. No. The Loyalty line is very common. It crosses the thumb ball horizontally.
7. Yes. Bars on all the fingertips show stress or endocrinal over-activity.
8. An Intensity line indicates restlessness and is a sign of someone that loves risk and adventure.
9. It's unlikely. A person with an Allergy line will almost certainly suffer from allergies of some form or another.

this can be terrifying, particularly as most keep their confusions, insecurities and fears well hidden. Don't read anyone's palm unless you're invited. Be diplomatic. Be gentle. Be kind.

Looking behind the veil

Don't be surprised to find that people are nothing like their outer personalities. Always trust what you read on the palm and not what you see of the person. Many of us have no idea of who we really are and we may be extremely defensive when our inner confusions are uncovered. Those with long peacock digits and short mirror fingers are particular good at hiding behind a mask. Adolescents can also be particularly difficult, because to them, image is all-important. They want to be seen as cool, wild and zany and will often blatantly deny that they are, for example, actually responsible, sensitive or confused.

Cover everything

Always read a palm by going through *all* the palm qualities as you've covered them in this book. I need hardly remind you that you ignore anything average, but I will anyway. There are ten points to check, always. These are: the thumb ball, skin texture, thumb length, thumb stiffness, finger length, finger stiffness, finger and thumb print patterns, palm print patterns, major lines, minor lines (including the subsidiary markings).

So always start with the thumb ball and work through the skin texture, then examine the thumb, then look for a particularly long or short finger, then check the print patterns, proceeding all the way through to the subsidiary lines. Don't jump straight to any one point. Measure all the other features in sequence, always.

Everyone has at least one interesting and unusual quality to their palms and usually there are three or four. It's by balancing these against *all the other qualities observed* that captures their unique individuality.

Let's say a person has a radial loop in their mirror finger (this means, as you know, they're hyper-receptive and extremely open to the influence of others). This is a hugely important marker, but you need to balance this against other qualities you observe. This individual may also have a long mirror finger for instance, and a strong thumb with silk skin. This makes them hyper-receptive to the influence of others (radial loop), deeply sensitive to the atmosphere around them (skin quality), bossy, idealistic, self-reflective (long mirror finger), strong-willed person (strong thumb). This is completely different to someone with a radial loop on their mirror finger that has grainy skin, a weak, bendy thumb and a short mirror finger. This would make a person hyper-receptive to the influence of others (radial loop), active and not particularly sensitive to their immediate atmosphere (skin quality), an easily-led individual who lacks self control (weak thumb) and who doubts themselves hugely (short mirror finger). So, though both these people are defined by their radial loop prints on their mirror fingers, it's the *other* qualities you observe alongside that makes a complete picture.

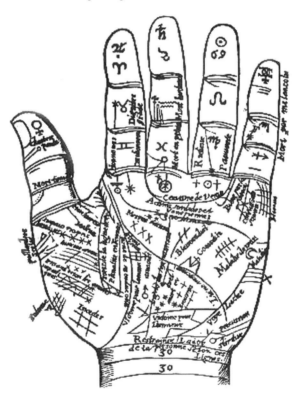

It all adds up...

Usually, the markings on the palm reinforce each other. For instance, a person with a major line that completely crosses the palm (obsessive) will have a lot of stress lines on their thumb ball and on their fingertips. They'll also have fairly stiff fingers. These points reinforce the signs of tension and the certainty that the person is a fixated, highly stressed, single-minded character. Always try to link your observations together in this way.

Or maybe it doesn't

Sometimes though, people have contradictory qualities. Human beings are complex and it's explaining the contradictions of personality that makes a reading wonderfully helpful. For instance, someone may have whorl patterns on every one of their fingers (this makes an inventive individualist, a non-conformist, someone that needs space) yet they might have a tied Line of Consciousness (meaning the beginning of this line doesn't part with the line of vitality). So, though they're naturally independent, needful of space and original (whorl patterns on all fingers) they've been dominated by a parent or some influence that makes them extremely cautious and unsure of their own ideas. They therefore lack the independence of mind that they naturally embody.

These kinds of contradictions come up all the time and by having them explained, people often make huge breakthroughs. They can suddenly see why they've always been frustrated and can make the changes they've always secretly wanted to make. Often revealing a person through reading their palm is like giving them permission to be themselves. It can be an intoxicating, liberating experience.

Think of the thumb

Whatever interesting points you find in the palm and fingers, always check the thumbs to find out how much self-control and strength of will a person has. Whatever quality you observe, be it obsession, jealousy or insecurity, the thumb's strength will tell you what 'grip' they have over it. A weak thumb makes a person much more at the mercy of their inner drives and more prone to give in to their weaknesses. If a person has, for instance, very flexible fingers, (easily distracted, open minded, poor concentration) but a strong thumb, they'll be able to keep their lack of focus in check.

Left and right

Absolutely always compare the active and passive palms. Anything interesting you see in one palm must be checked against the other. See if what is in the developed, mature, outer personality is also in the inner, passive personality. Look for any features that change from one palm to another. The line qualities you see that get stronger from passive to active show positive development. If a line gets stronger on the active hand, it shows someone's worked hard to develop the qualities they may have lacked. For instance, a person may have a weak, short Vitality Line on their passive palm and a strong, complete line on their active hand. This means that though they've had an insecure upbringing with low vitality and they've found it hard to feel secure, they are building or have built (depending on their age) a strong foundation for themselves. They're able to support themselves, they've got plenty of vitality, they've developed a sense of permanence and will or can create a secure household and family.

When you find (as you often will) contradictory *print* patterns, from passive to active palms, then you have a person permanently different in their intimate, passive and private selves than in their active professional lives. For instance, a person may have a whorl on the mirror finger of the passive hand and a loop on the mirror finger of the active palm. This means they'll be perfectly flexible and normal in their outward interaction with others. However, privately they'll need to have space for themselves, they'll see themselves as different and will be more quirky and individual.

Every marking you see you must compare the active and passive hand and see if it's repeated or contradicted.

The wonder of it all

Everything you see on the palm is good and bad. You could describe a person's very short mirror finger as a sign of a crippling sense of inadequacy and zero self-esteem. You could also say they had nurturing issues with their mother figure and they are refreshingly lacking in egoism and self-obsession. Don't put negative points too bluntly, try to be diplomatic.

When you have to point out a negative feature, a short Vitality Line, for instance, do point out the positive side as well. A person with short Vitality Lines may be insecure and unstable, but they are highly mobile and adaptable and can easily adjust to new lifestyles. A person with composite patterns on their thumbs may dither terribly about the big decisions in life, but they are wonderfully understanding of others. Always try to be uplifting and optimistic in your judgments. Always be generous to the person you're reading to, but be honest. Don't skirt the difficult issues – they also must be passed on.

Growing, knowing and listening

From now on, try to get as much experience of palm study as you can. Never fail to get the print of anyone with an interesting palm.

You'll find your intuition will develop as you get into the process of palmistry. Do pass on any visions or feelings you get, but don't forget the vital insights that palmistry reveals are far more important than the sense you have that the lady in front of you has a cat named George or a blue bedroom!

As a palmist, people will open to you. You'll find clients confessing all sorts of terrible secrets – the termination they had as a teenager, the affair they had last summer, their secret hatred of their wife's mother. The palmist's consultation room is a private, almost holy place – in many ways we are the modern replacement for the priest's confessional. Be a good listener. Never display shock at what you're told, never judge or condemn, never pass on or betray anyone's privacy, no matter what your personal views are.

It's easy as a palmist to wander into the role of life authority, making people's minds up for them. If someone tells you their partner is unfaithful and abusive and that they want to leave, it's not your role to tell them to do so. You can only point out the stress they may be suffering or the new beginning indicated by the renewed section of their Vitality Line. You are charged with giving as much insight as possible into the person's inner drives, needs and motivations, but that's all. What use people make of that information is up to them.

Secret palmist assignment

Take the palm prints of five people you know only vaguely. Measure their thumb ball and skin texture and the stiffness of their fingers.

Go home and work through all the levels of analysis, compare the active and passive hands constantly and make a note of their differences. Look to see what's getting stronger and what's getting weaker. Look for differences in finger length and fingerprint pattern between the palms. When you find a feature that's important: a line that's particularly short or one that's extra long; an interesting print or a digit longer than average, put all the other qualities you observe alongside, to make a rounded picture of that person. When you've written up your notes on each person, pass them onto your 'clients'. Take a note of their feedback.

Brain bashing quiz
Time given: ten minutes

1. Is it OK to read someone's palm even if they haven't given you permission?
2. Is it good practice to read only one feature on its own?
3. Should you start a reading by looking at the lines?
4. Should you read only the active palm?
5. Do the indications on the palm always tend to agree with each other?
6. When you read a palm, should you make people's decisions for them?
7. Is intuition more important than analysis of the palm signs?
8. Does a floppy thumb mean a person is in control of their fate?
9. When you point out a negative feature, should you blame it on a person's karma?

Answers are on the next page.

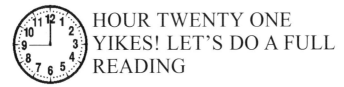

HOUR TWENTY ONE
YIKES! LET'S DO A FULL
READING

Going the whole nine yards

In this chapter you're going to read a pair of palms, recording everything that strikes you as notable about the personality. Don't panic, you'll be guided slowly through the whole process. You'll simply go through the palms exactly as you've learned to do in this book, disregarding anything average and building a profile of the individual. It's not going to be as difficult as you may think!

Examine these palms carefully. This person is right handed. The skin quality is grainy, and the fingers are of average flexibility. The thumbs are stiff with simple arch prints on them. The thumb balls are full and firm.

Step by step

OK. So let's start with the basics. What does the big thumb ball tell us about the person's vitality? Does this person have low energy

---

Answers

1. No. Palmistry is too penetrating and intimate to be performed without permission.
2. No. Any feature you observe must be considered alongside everything else.
3. No. Start with the thumb ball and work through everything.
4. No. Always read both passive and active palms.
5. No. People often display contradictory personality traits.
6. No. You must let your clients make their own decisions.
7. No. The indications observed on the palm are much more important than intuitive glimpses.
8. No. A floppy thumb indicates vulnerability to exterior forces in life.
9. No. You should balance any negative point with a positive slant, or with a beneficial characteristic.

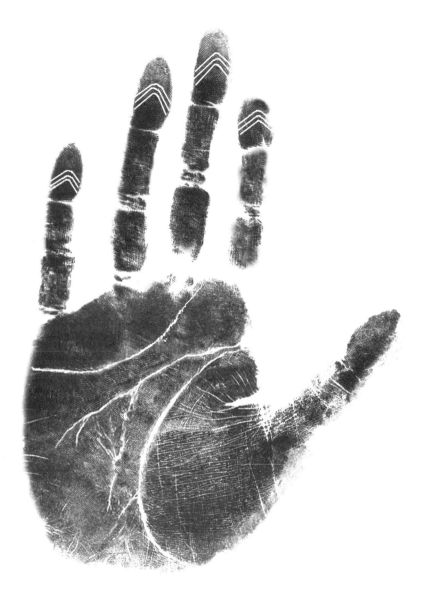

resources?

Next, the grainy skin quality. Is grainy skin the sign of a hyper-sensitive person or someone that thrives on activity and stimulus? Make your decision now!

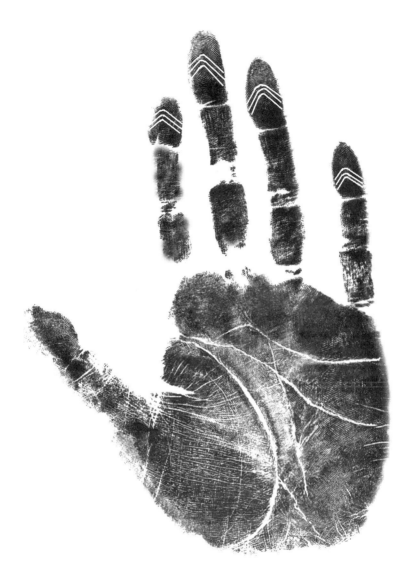

Digging into the digits

Let's look at the digits now, including the thumbs. What exceptional qualities can you pick out here? Massive clue – the thumbs, mirror and peacock digits on both hands are definitely *not* of average length. Which are exceptionally long and which short?

Starting with the thumb, work out the qualities this long or short one would give – does he or she have adequate self-control? Can this person keep a tight grip on themselves, or are they self-indulgent and easy-going?

Look at the mirror fingers. What do they tell you about the person's relationship with their mother figure and their self-esteem?

Now the peacock digits; is this person likely to be a larger-than-life personality? Would he or she have a drive to perform? To display themselves to others? Would they be flirtatious and want to take risks? Remember that the greater the difference between the mirror and peacock digits' length, the greater the difference between outer public and inner private personality.

Probing the print patterns

OK, now for the dermatoglyphics. Here we have a very rare case, someone with *ten* simple arches. This is a vital aspect of this person's character. Do you remember learning how simple arches resemble layers of soil, repressing, burying, and fixing? Would this create a mind-set that is freedom-loving, inventive, or conventional? Does this pattern put them in tune with the modern world? Would they be flexible, intuitive and expressive?

Looking at the lines

As there are no print patterns on the palm itself, we can go on to examine the major lines. Check the Vitality Line – does this person have a lot of vitality? Do they have strong roots and a firm sense of place? What does the one on the passive palm say about the stability of their upbringing and family life? How do the Vitality

Lines on the active and passive palms compare?

Put the characteristics of the Vitality Line and the thumb ball mount together with the skin quality and see what you get!

Now examine the Line of Emotion. Is this person romantic, expressive, idealistic, or a sociopath? What does the active palm's Line of Emotion say about the person's ability to express their traditional gender role? This is a massive clue! Compare the two lines of emotion and describe the difference between the inner and outer emotional states.

OK. Now for the Line of Consciousness. Look at the one on the active hand, which crosses the palm completely – what does this mean? Is this person level-headed or subjective? How do they think – logically or intuitively? Do they think a lot? Do they have a mind that applies knowledge or one that ponders over many possibilities? How does this line affect spontaneity? Compare this line with the one on the passive hand. What does this tell you about the difference between the person's inner and outer personalities?

The separateness of the beginning of the Line of Consciousness and Vitality Line tells you about the separateness of this person from their roots and family and their willingness to trust their own ideas. Is this person adventurous? Do they inhabit a similar mental framework to their parents?

The Lifepath Line is next. It's fairly strong, but ragged throughout its length. What does this tell you? The beginning of this line is in the Sea of Subconscious. Will this person have a conventional, structured career, based on the need for security and the demands of the family?

Now the minor lines. There's little in the way of these, except for travel lines branching off the base of the Vitality Lines on both palms. What does this mean?

Now put all the points you've worked through together and see what you've got!

Summing up

Looking at the large, firm thumb ball, the clear, strong Vitality Line and the extra-long thumbs on both hands, it's easy to see a personality bursting with drive and lusty energy, with good self-control. This is a physical person with loads of drive, who will be able to push themselves relentlessly to achieve their goals.

The skin texture is grainy, which is more common on men's hands. It shows a need for activity and stimulus and is not an indicator of enormous sensitivity.

Moving on to the fingers, the mirror digit is tiny and the peacock digit huge. The mother figure rewarded attention-seeking behavior, as a child there was little opportunity of considering his/her real needs and responsibilities. He/she has extremely low self-esteem and this will give a reluctance to present him/herself to the world as he/she is; he/she feels unworthy. This person doubts their own achievements, no matter how successful. He/she is likely to suffer self-neglect, and will ignore his/her true needs. In one-to-one situations, this will be far more obvious than with crowds. This personality trait will have a strong impact on life experiences until it is understood and compensated for.

Now for the peacock finger. The digit being extra long is a predominantly male trait, as is grainy skin, so we may risk a guess that this is a man's hand. The long peacock means he'll hide deeper feelings behind the mask of a persona, and indulge in attention-seeking and a love of danger and excitement. Someone with a long peacock digit will always be a little larger than life. He's likely to have good presentation skills and to possess a well-developed sense of humor. All professional entertainers, sports people, artists and celebrities have a peacock finger of exaggerated length. He'll have a personal magnetism, and be attractive to the opposite sex.

This individual has a complete set of ten simple arch prints. He's highly repressed and unable to adapt to the modern world. Someone with a lot of simple arches is practical, stubborn, old-fashioned, often crude in their use of language, and they despise superficiality.

The Vitality Line we've already covered, so we'll do the Line of Consciousness. The one on the active palm is obsessive; it cuts off the Sea of Subconscious completely. Along with the simple arches, this is another sign of severe repression. It also shows single-mindedness and a lack of spontaneity. This person looks a long way into the future; they think a lot and can get obsessively fixated on their mental goals. The thinking process on both hands shows a slightly intuitive quality (as the lines drop downward). The line on the passive hand is not obsessive; it's more inward-looking and forked, showing diversity and a solitary childhood. It's only in their working, active life that this obsessive quality is enacted. The gap between the Line of Consciousness and the Vitality Line shows certain adventurousness and a willingness to trust one's own ideas.

The Lines of Emotion are clear and well formed, showing strongly accessed emotions, but the endings are very different. The one on the active hand drops downward, which shows possessiveness and a drive to express the feminine side (assuming this is a man's hand). The line on the passive hand shows a romantic idealist.

The Lifepath line is interesting; it's clear but ragged, showing someone trying too hard to make their mark on the world. Often highly successful people have Lifepath lines like this. The base of the line is in the Sea of Subconscious, so he bases his work on other people and uses social empathy in his career. The base of the line also indicates a distinct move away from parent-defined career paths.

The only minor lines are travel lines, showing a drive to travel and to connect to other places, cultures and experiences.

Analysis

This is a brief analysis so only the main points are considered here. There are three massively powerful personality traits that leap out at us from this palm. This person has tremendous energy, enormous repression and a strong drive to be on the public stage.

The thumb ball and Vitality Line indicate an irrepressible force of nature, a ball of energy, skillfully mastered by a strong thumb. The skin quality indicates a need for action.

The ten simple arch prints show a practical, stubborn person, at odds with the modern world and its superficiality. The prints repress all spontaneous emotional expression. Added to this is the completely crossing Line of Consciousness on the active palm which cuts off the Sea of Subconscious and the emotions.

The imbalance in between the mirror and peacock digits demonstrate an enormous drive to hide behind a mask and to display a persona to the world. This person would take risks and is likely to be perhaps a touch self-destructive. Also the Lifepath Line shows someone struggling to make their mark on the world. The beginning of the line indicates someone who works with the public and who's not living a lifestyle inherited from the parents. This is exaggerated by their adventurousness and separateness from their roots indicated by the separation of the Line of Consciousness and Vitality Lines and also the travel lines.

Next, the Line of Emotion has a deep downturn at its end on the active palm, which shows an ability to access a feminine side, perhaps to some comic or entertaining effect, given the huge peacock finger. This person is something of a romantic idealist passively.

The long, strong Vitality Lines show great energy, and a solid, stable background. There is a good connection to this individual's roots and he or she would be well-grounded and realistic. Looking at the short mirror fingers though, we know that though this person was given a secure upbringing, he/she was not encouraged to be her/himself.

Do you want to hazard a guess now as to who this might be?

Well, this is the palm of female impersonator, Barry Humphries, a.k.a. Dame Edna Everage. The persona he's created means he very rarely appears in public as himself. The old-fashioned, essentially music-hall act of the Dame, is bawdy and almost Hogarthian in his mocking, earthy humor. He attacks modern manners and pretentiousness and destroys any sense of pretentious high culture. What stands out in his act is Barry's tremendous energy. There have been times in life when he's been self destructive and it's a little-known fact that he has refined emotional and artistic tastes in his private life.

Secret palmist assignment

We've only covered Barry Humphries's palm in brief. Go through the two palms again and see what else you can pick up about him.

Whenever you come across the palms of celebrities in magazines and books, use your palmistry skills to decipher any clues you can to the person's upbringing and inner personality.

Brain bashing quiz
Time given: ten minutes

1. In Barry Humphries's prints, what characteristic informs you of a stable, secure childhood?
2. What is the primary indicator of Barry's larger-than-life personality?
3. What marking shows an inclination to display opposite-gender behavior?
4. What marking shows a mind set that is old-fashioned, stubborn, repressive and out of step with the modern world?
5. What sign would you look for on a hand to show someone is working too hard to make their mark on the world?
6. What does the short mirror finger tell you about Barry's relationship with himself and his achievements?
7. What in Barry's hands shows an abundance of vitality?
8. What shows Barry's lifestyle and work choice is different from his parents and that he works with the public?
9. What sign shows a desire to travel and to seek out new experiences?

Answers are on the next page.

HOUR TWENTY TWO
PASSIONATE PALMISTRY

Love lines

Most people that come to you for a reading will be seeking advice and guidance on their love-life. We'll take a look at the emotional and sexual side of a reading here.

Hot to trot?

What signs should you look for to check if someone is a passionate person? Well, that's easy. The signs of a red-hot-lover are easy to spot. Remember though, the lustier a person is, the less likely they are to be faithful!

Firstly, the thumb ball has to be measured. If it's firm, warm and springy, the person will have lots of physical oomph in their engine and a lusty sex drive. If it's flat and flabby, however wild their fantasies are, they may not have the energy to live them out.

Take a look at the Vitality Line. If it's strong and long, the

---

Answers

1. A stable childhood is shown by the clear, strong, unbroken Vitality Lines.
2. The massive relative length of the peacock digit indicates a larger than life personality.
3. The down-turned ending of the Line of Emotion on the active palm indicates opposite gender behavior.
4. The high number of simple arch fingerprints.
5. The frazzled, scratchy quality of the Lifepath Line.
6. No matter how successful he is, he'll feel inadequate and under-confident when he's being himself.
7. The full, firm, thumb balls and the clear, strong lines of vitality.
8. His Lifepath Lines start in the Sea of Subconscious area.
9. The travel lines branching off the base of the Vitality Lines.

person will have oodles of sexual stamina and good vitality. If it's weak and broken, they may be a touch cool and run out of steam fairly quickly.

The next aspect to examine is the quality of the Line of Emotion. If it's deep, red and curves upward to end between the mirror and wall digits, and if it's without breaks or islands, the person will be romantic and will demonstrate emotions strongly. A straight, red line won't be so demonstrative nor so romantic but will certainly get worked up quickly. If the line's broken and weak, the emotions are more turbulent and weaker, the person won't

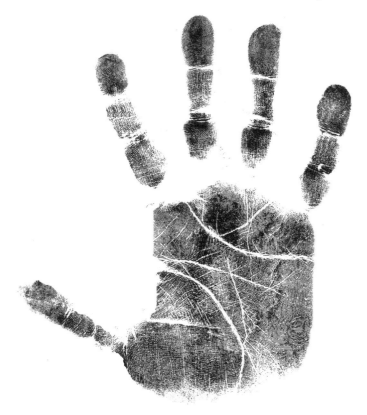

A palm with all the signs of strong passion potential

know exactly what they're feeling or why.

Look for a passion line. If there's one present, this will give a lively sexual imagination, they may be into role-playing, and dressing up.

Examine the balance between the mirror and peacock finger's lengths. A long peacock finger is notoriously flirtatious, playful and keen to display themselves in a favorable light. They'll make an effort to please, flatter and adorn themselves. A long mirror-fingered person wants to be taken seriously and won't want to dress up or play games.

The length of the antenna finger will give a good indication of communication skills. Bear in mind, sex is a basic form of communication. A long antenna finger will have a more varied technique, a larger vocabulary and more ability to talk the language of love. A short finger will be less skilled in their range, depth and technique in the bedroom department.

Compatibility

Comparing the palms of two people to see if they're compatible is something you'll often get asked to do. Here's how.

Sensitivity and Atmosphere

One of the most important areas of romantic compatibility is the skin texture. People with widely differing palm skin textures never get along. The lady with silk skin will find the guy with coarse skin oafish, thick-skinned and insensitive. He would find her a drippy, over-fastidious neurotic.

Skin texture tells us about the kind of circumstances, environment and ambiance that is appropriate for a person, romantically speaking.

A person with silk skin texture responds to subtlety above all: candlelight, whispered conversation, innuendo, the most gentle of caresses.

A person with paper skin would like conversation, wit, and a sense of intelligence in their love play. They'd respond readily to body language and eye signals. The environment ideally would be partially lit, with background music and a light, airy atmosphere.

Grainy-skinned people wouldn't want to linger too long in love games, they haven't got the patience! They prefer a sense of urgency in their romantic assignations. They love to *do* things with a partner, preferably something exciting, stimulating and fun: a rollercoaster ride, a drive in an open-top sports car, a visit to a night-club. They respond to provocative, fashionable clothing and good light. They like unambiguous signals of desire: touching, kissing, and teasing.

Coarse skinned people won't respond to anything subtle. The direct approach is by far the best. This type won't spend time lingering over the words of love or poetry. The way to get close to a man with this skin type is in a shared meal, a country walk, or perhaps doing something outdoors together, to prove you're as tough as he is (coarse skin is much more likely to be found on a man's palm). If all else fails, you may have to simply take him by the hand and drag him off to bed!

Who's boss?

In long-term relationships the issue of dominance has to be considered. Relationships are about working through life's problems together and it's not healthy if one dominates the other too much.

The key issue to check is the length of the mirror fingers. If one has an extra-long mirror digit and the other has an extra-short one, you can bet your bottom dollar the long mirror-fingered one is boss. The trouble is, while the long peacock fingered person is being reckless and irresponsible, it's the long mirror-fingered partner that's doing all the worrying and clearing up the mess. And when the long mirror finger gets all self-obsessed and control-freaky, the long peacock-fingered soul is mopping their fevered brow, obeying their every whim, while feeling this whole 'me' trip is a trifle self-indulgent.

Compatibility works best when both individuals have mirror fingers of similar relative length, i.e. both short, medium or long.

Fingerprint comparison

The print patterns are extremely important in relationships. In long-term relationships, it's the prints on the *passive* palm that count. On first meeting a person you get to know them through their active palm. True intimacy means connecting with the deeper, passive personality as shown by the passive hand.

Mirror finger print patterns

The prints on the passive hand's mirror finger are by far the most important. Ordinary lunar loops tend to get along with anyone and are highly flexible. Anything different though, is important.

On the mirror finger, a whorl print means a person can never see themselves as part of a unit. They'll always have a sense of being an individual, they need the space to be alone. This can be a problem if their partner has, for instance, a deeply insecure *radial loop* pattern on their corresponding digit. The radial loop person is always looking for re-assurance that they're needed, but a whorl mirror-fingered person may too easily close themselves off.

A whorl-fingered character tends to be self-centered, they like to put themselves in the middle of their own world. This is the opposite of the composite pattern. People with composites have trouble knowing what they want and are always indecisive about personal decisions. They may find a person with a whorl selfish and unable to compromise; the whorl-fingered person may see them as dithering procrastinators.

A simple arch on the mirror finger will naturally repress their emotions and won't find it easy to express their needs. It may take a long time before they confess their love, or hurt, or yearning. This print can also give a practical inclination, so they may not be impressed with a partner that can't wire a plug.

If an individual with a simple arch is matched with one with a *tented arch*, frustration will result. A tented arch on the mirror finger makes one intense, demonstrative and excitement-seeking. Such a person would be driven crazy by the repressive, practical quality of the simple arch.

Thumb print patterns

On the thumb, a whorl is always keen to show off their independence, so don't be surprised if your partner has this pattern and they decide they want to go to the party alone. It's not that they don't love you; it's simply that they have to be seen to be free. A person with a simple arch here would be happy to talk about the extension to the kitchen they're planning all evening, while the soul with the composite pattern on their thumb would be desperate to know what the hell they should do with the rest of their lives. Generally, having different patterns on the thumbs is less difficult than having opposing ones on the mirror digits.

Other indications to consider

Other patterns to check for in an emotional and sexual comparison are the lines of emotion and the affection lines.

Examine the Line of Emotion to see the quality of a person's emotional drive. A weak, short line shows weak, short-lived emotional connections; a strong long line shows the opposite. Pay particular attention to the *end* of the Line of Emotion. This shows whether a person is idealistic (ending at the mirror finger), jealous (dropping to the Vitality Line), romantic (ending between the mirror and wall digits), obsessive (very long), reclusive (very short) or flirtatious (ending in lots of little lines).

Now examine the affection lines. This gives an indication of negative patterns locked in the subconscious, a fixation with an ideal partner (a very long line), a drive to seek out difficult partners (a divorce line) or there may be a line that cuts off the antenna digit (long periods of sexual abstinence).

Finally, check the setting of the antenna digit, if it's low set, this gives sexual immaturity and father parent issues.

When you've checked all these points, you can give an excellent emotional and sexual analysis that will leave your clients stunned. Go to it!

Secret palmist assignment

Take the palm prints of five people you don't know. Measure their thumb ball and skin texture and carefully note their dermatoglyphics.

Go home and work through all the levels of an emotional

and sexual analysis, work out their general lustiness and their sensitivity. Examine their lines of emotion particularly carefully. When you've written up your notes on each person, sit down with them and give them a reading. Get the person who you're reading for to contribute, ask them questions, get their feedback.

Brain bashing quiz
Time given: ten minutes

1. What points do you check to see if a person is passionate?
2. How does skin quality factor in a couple's emotional compatibility?
3. Would someone with silk skin connect with a person with coarse skin?
4. Would you check the size of the thumbs to look for dominating personalities?
5. If a person has a whorl print on their passive mirror finger, would they get along with someone that has a composite on the same digit?
6. What about a person with a tented arch on the passive mirror finger - would they be compatible with someone with a simple arch in the same place?
7. What sign indicates a person is flirtatious?
8. Is a low-set antenna digit important in an emotional analysis?
9. Does a very long, straight, affection line indicate lifelong celibacy?

   swers are on the next page.

HOUR TWENTY THREE
LINES OF WORK -
VOCATIONAL PALMISTRY

Talking business

You can give useful help when people ask you what job they should do – it's a question that'll get put to you frequently. Never recommend a specific job though. To say: 'you should be an architect', is too simplistic. You can only ever point to a particular *field* of work.

The word vocation comes from the Greek 'voca', to call. This is the true nature of work – a calling to which a person is particularly suited and for which they have a gift. It is in this sense that palmistry gives guidance about job choice – not as the best way to accrue a high salary, but to locate the field where a person will find satisfaction and fulfillment.

Answers

1. Points to check are: thumb ball, Vitality Line, Line of Emotion, passion line (if present), length of the peacock and antenna digits.
2. Skin texture is about the circumstances, environment and ambience that is appropriate for a person, romantically speaking.
3. No. Their differing palm skin means their levels of sensitivity are vastly different.
4. No. The mirror fingers' lengths are checked for dominance.
5. It could be difficult. A whorl gives a strong sense of being an individual, a composite an open, undecided personality.
6. These two people aren't compatible; one is cautious and repressed, the other excitable and intense.
7. A spray of fine lines at the end of the Line of Emotion.
8. Yes. Low set antenna digits show sexual maturity and father issues.
9. No. It shows an exhaustive search for the 'right' partner.

Begin with the skin

Always start a vocational analysis with the skin. Silk-skinned folk want work that is gentle and non competitive; they need a calm atmosphere and are best suited to the arts, therapy and caring professions. Paper-skinned people seek a work environment where there's an exchange of ideas, where paper and the tools of communication are present. Grainy-skinned people get bored easily, so they need goals and targets and the thrill of competition. They work hard and can do practically anything as long as it doesn't require too much sensitivity and it doesn't bore them. Coarse-skinned folk want manual work and they love to be outdoors. Sedentary, desk-bound work would drive them crazy.

Clear and simple

As a rule, a clear simple palm with few lines on it, likes a simple, straightforward form of work without complexity, confusion or too much variety, where a full palm likes a buzzy, changeable and mentally complex working world.

Put your finger on it

Now check the digits. The thumb is considered first. Someone with a stiff thumb can push themselves hard, they don't need much supervision. A bendy thumbed person may not be too highly motivated when the going gets tough. Bendy thumbs suit 'people' professions, stiff ones suit work where a hard slog is required.

Then look at the mirror fingers. A long mirror digit needs to be the boss of their working arena; they like to be in control. They want work with a lot of personal input, like self-employment, people management, self-development, or a mothering role, like

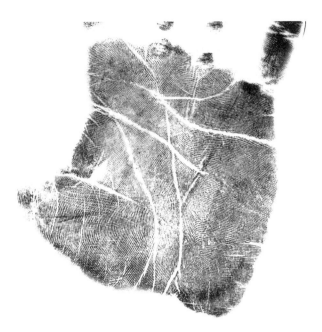

Simple palm of a mechanic, and below Complex palm of a psychoanalyst

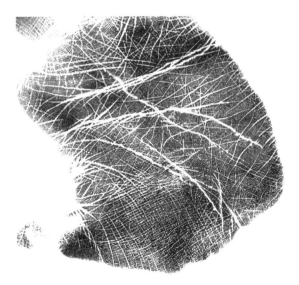

teaching or caring. Work for them always has an emphasis on being respected, implementing high standards, and expecting high quality and fulfillment of personal ideals. They're also drawn to all self-reflective pursuits: psychology, counseling, self-development, astrology – anything related to the arts of looking into others.

The wall digit is considered next. If it's long, the person would like to work within bureaucratic structures, implementing rules, regulations, boundaries and laws. Any governmental or large organization will suit, where they can check, file, measure, plan and research.

If this finger's short or bent, the person will be unconventional, they'll want work that challenges authority, or one with a sense of variety, without routine. People that work in the travel industry often have this sign on their palms.

If the peacock finger is long, a person wants to demonstrate a skill or show off in some way or use a mask to create a persona to work with. This can be highly effective in the arts, in people professions and anywhere one needs to get behind a public image i.e. sales or politics.

The antenna digit is important in work, if it's long, anything with a slant towards communication skills: teaching, writing, selling and advising will be a good outlet. Don't forget an antenna digit can be long but look short if it's low set.

Working out the prints

Now for the dermatoglyphics. The patterns on the active hand's wall finger are important for work choice. If there's a whorl print here, a person will choose freedom over worldly success. They like to work in a niche profession where they can do their own thing, in their own time. A simple arch on the wall finger gives a drive for work that's secure, conventional and financially rewarding.

On the mirror finger, a whorl wants autonomy, a simple arch practicality and a radial loop wants work in the caring, 'people' professions. Tented arches want a dash of drama and excitement. Innovative teaching and motivating others is a gift they possess.

The markings *between* the digits are very important. A loop of leisure means a person wants pleasure from their work and will often make a job of their hobby. They'll prioritize their leisure time, lacking the dedication for an all-consuming, serious profession like law or medicine. A loop of industry is the opposite pattern, giving a strong sense of taking work deadly seriously with a willingness to give up leisure time.

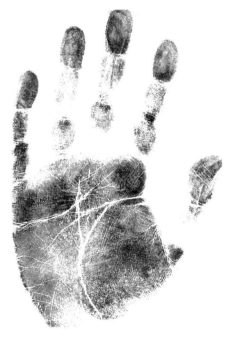

Working lines

The Lifepath Line is the most important for work. You'll get most requests about work choice from folk without this line. As you know, this means a person hasn't defined themselves and they don't know what they want to really do with themselves. Don't advise people with **The hand of a banker – note Lifepath Line joined to the Vitality Line, also the long wall digit** no Lifepath Line to go self-employed. Self employment requires clearly defined goals, a sense of structure and dedication. A person with no Lifepath Line lacks these qualities.

Where the Lifepath Line *is* present, a line from the Sea of Subconscious area is inclined towards artistic, personal and social-based work, where one from the Vitality Line is drawn to more traditional, structured and institution-bound work. A Lifepath Line joined to the Vitality Line means vocation is about the demands of family, security and tradition and not about personal enjoyment. Often a new line begins in the centre of the palm, signifying a time when a new set of goals and working priorities are taken on board. Don't forget that the more stressed and scratchy the Lifepath Line is, the more a person tends to be stressed and striving to find worldly, not personal success. They need to slow down and re-frame their priorities. A long, strong, deep line will mean a person is content with what they do, even if they're a grave digger. They will always find balance and establish goals for themselves eventually.

Look at the Line of Consciousness. A short line here means a person will want to apply what they know in *doing* something; they'll want to channel all their energies into a particular skill. A long Line of Consciousness wants to consider, speculate, learn and evaluate. A long line is good at giving their own opinion and working things out for themselves. Generally, a long Line of Consciousness is more suited to working with abstract information.

Work that needs independence of thought and initiative suits a person with a large gap at the beginning of their Vitality Line and the Line of Consciousness. A person with both lines tied together here wouldn't be very good at making their own decisions, they need to do a job where there's a procedure to follow.

The Line of Emotion is a great indicator of how much an individual wants to integrate with people at work. A team worker or a manager needs to have a good Line of Emotion so they can connect to others. A person with a short Line of Emotion won't be able to relate to others very well – they'll function better working alone. A person with a very long Line of Emotion often is drawn to work in the caring professions.

Minor lines at work

The minor lines often give clues to particular professions – wherever you see one of the following markings, it indicates a gift for a particular realm of work. The Ring of Solomon, for instance is often found on palmists, readers and counselors, so a skill in insightful, one-to-one work is found. The teacher's square is common on all those who teach and manage others. Samaritan lines are common on care workers and healers, and a traveler's fork at the base of the Vitality Line is extremely common on airline pilots, holiday reps and the like. Someone with a Fantasy line likes to use their imagination at work, in, for instance, designing clothes or teaching drama. The loop of nature is an indication of someone that loves to work with growing things and a fine, straight, Nervous Activity line is a sign of a person that needs to use their capacity for ideas.

Remember, don't try to narrow a person down to a single profession, just assign a particular area of work. This is enough to get people going in the right direction.

Secret palmist assignment

Take the palm prints of five people you don't know. Measure their thumb stiffness, thumb ball size and skin texture and carefully note their dermatoglyphics.

Go home and work through all the levels of a vocational analysis. Try to guess what field of work the people you're examining might do. Remember the thumb's stiffness is important; people with bendy thumbs don't like to push themselves too hard. Examine their Lifepath Lines particularly carefully. When you've written up your notes on each person, sit down with them and give them a reading. Get the person who you're reading for to contribute, ask them what they do and what they'd like to do if they could work at any job. Listen to their feedback.

Brain bashing quiz
Time given: ten minutes

1. Where does the word 'vocation' originate?
2. Should you begin a vocational analysis with the dermatoglyphics?
3. What does a long mirror-fingered person want from work?
4. Does a long peacock-fingered person love responsibility?
5. Would you find a person with a long antenna digit as a writer?
6. Does a person with a radial loop on their mirror finger seek a competitive working environment?
7. What about a simple arch on the mirror finger? Would they

want to inspire others?

8. What's the most important major line in terms of work?

9. Does a Lifepath Line beginning tied to the Vitality Line mean a person works with the public?

Answers are on the next page.

HOUR TWENTY FOUR
PSYCHOLOGICAL PALMISTRY

Psyching people out

In many ways you could say that any palm reading is an in-depth psychological analysis. The power of modern palmistry is that you have in the palm, a map of every nuance and tributary in a person's thinking processes.

Print power

The print patterns are particularly powerful in terms of psychology. By simply explaining a single observation, like a set of simple arches, a radial loop, or a composite, you can free people from life-long patterns of behavior. When you explain that a person's whorl patterns, for instance, means they find group situations difficult, that they must have space, that they must work everything out for themselves, you're allowing them to be themselves for the first time. People have no idea why they are a certain way and give themselves a hard time because they're not like everyone else.

Answers

1. The word 'vocation' is from the Greek 'voca', - 'to call'.
2. No. Begin a vocational analysis with the skin texture.
3. Long mirror-fingered people want control, respect and personal input. At work they have high standards and personal ideals.
4. No. A long peacock-fingered person avoids responsibility if at all possible.
5. Yes. A long antenna is common on writer's palms.
6. No. Radial looped folk hate competition and seek a supportive environment.
7. No. Simple arched souls seek practicality, security and stability.
8. The Lifepath Line is the most significant for vocation.
9. No. This pattern means they work in a traditional profession, with structure, family and security as the primary drives in employment.

When you point out their particular palm patterns, you're pointing out the missing piece of the jigsaw puzzle of their souls.

Seeing and revealing

A palm reading is like describing the lens a person sees the world through, with all its distortions, warps and shades. The process opens people's eyes and makes them see themselves and the world differently. The words of help and advice you give them will stay with them always. That's why giving good palm readings is the most rewarding job in the world.

Let's look at a few palms and pick out some psychological traits.

Extrovert or introvert

This is probably the most important distinction of per-sonality and there are obvious differences between the two types on the palm.

Introverted people tend to keep their fingers closed tightly together, they can't open up easily. The skin quality is often either silk or coarse. The lines are faint and fine or thick and trench-like. The Line of Consciousness curves deeply into the Sea of Subconscious, showing an inward-focused

The palm of an introvert

mentality. The Line of Consciousness is likely to be tied to the beginning of the Vitality Line. A long mirror finger can also add to the quality of introversion.

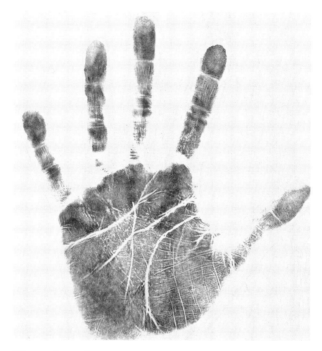

The palm of an extrovert

Extroverts naturally hold their fingers widely spread. They often have grainy skin and a long peacock finger. The Line of Consciousness is straight and the lines are generally strong and bold. In particular, there's a large gap between the beginning of the Line of Consciousness and the Vitality Line.

Obsessive or open-minded

Let's look at some more personality types. Another important distinction is that of the narrow minded, obsessive and the free-thinking, flexible personality.

The classic sign of the obsessive is a simian line. Narrow-minded people may also have a Line of Consciousness and a Line of Emotion that run very close together or they may have lots of lines joining the two. Other signs to look for are very stiff fingers and a lot of whorl print patterns.

The classic sign for an open person is actually ten ulna (normal)

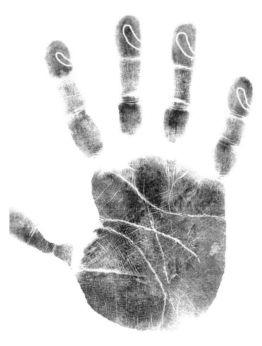

The palm of an open personality

loops on the fingers, showing an easy-going, sociable, flexible person. Composite patterns on the thumbs or mirror fingers also tend to make a person open to all perspectives.

Other signs of flexibility are fingers that are very flexible and major lines that curve slightly. To be truly open-minded, it's important that no lines completely cross the palm from one side to the other.

Psychological meltdown

What about the signs of mental breakdown, how does this show on the palm? Well, this is fortunately rare but easy to spot.

The Line of Consciousness is obviously vital in this respect – an island or numerous breaks on this line are indicative of potential breakdown. Also, it's problematic if this line's weak and poorly formed or if it curves very deeply into the Sea of

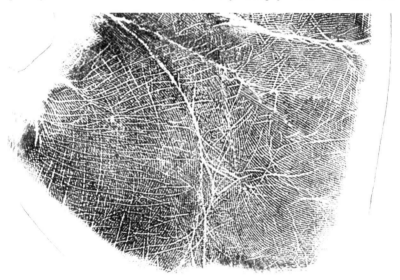

The palm of a person that's suffered numerous mental break-downs

Subconscious.

An obvious sign of mental fragility is a full hand with a multitude of lines. This indicates extreme stress, particularly if there are lines on the fingertips as well as on the palm itself. If there is no Lifepath Line present (as in the last illustration), or if it's a very poorly formed line, a person tends to be much more unstable in life generally.

One more indication to look for in an erratic mentality is a very strong fantasy line.

Bear in mind that the lines change and none of these problems are necessarily permanent.

Low self-esteem

One of the most crippling psychological conditions is low self-esteem. This is extremely easy to see in the palm.

The number one indicator of self-esteem problems is of course the short mirror finger. This attribute is exaggerated if the mirror fingers on both passive and active palms are significantly short. This makes the peacock finger relatively long, and with it a persona is usually developed. However loud the outer personality though, the actual private self-esteem is low. Other signs which exaggerate or give this quality are: radial loops on both mirror fingers; a weak or short Vitality Line; a strongly tied beginning of the Line of Consciousness to the Vitality Line, and a weak or poorly formed Lifepath Line.

Repression

We live in an age where we're encouraged to 'let it all hang out' – self expression is very much the order of the day. However much they're invited though, some people remain a closed book, holding their feelings in, no matter what.

The signs to look for are: a lot of simple arch prints on the digits (particularly on both mirror digits); a Line of Consciousness that crosses the palm completely; a simian line; a simple arch print in the Sea of Subconscious area of the palm; very stiff fingers or a Line of Emotion that's very short or one that crosses the palm completely.

Anti-authoritarian

The classic outcast that rages against society is marked most often by a short wall finger.

Other signs are: a whorl on this digit or lots of whorls generally;

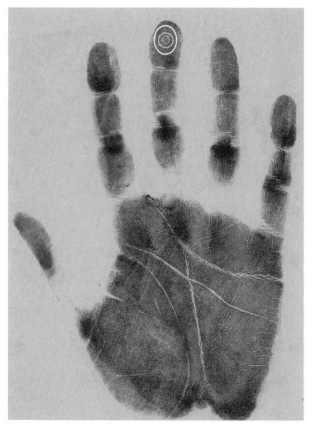

The hand of the editor of a Marxist newspaper

a very strong Lifepath Line, stronger than the other lines on the palm; a very strong fantasy line; a very long Line of Consciousness or a whorl in the Sea of Subconscious area of the palm.

Learning disabilities

A person with moderate to severe leaning difficulties will indicate this with a very weak, very short, or poorly formed Line of Consciousness. If there are very few, thick, scar-like lines on the palm, this is often an indication of a low IQ. A simian line on a very simple palm is another indication. It's worth noting that a Line of Consciousness that crosses the palm from side to side is indicative of dyslexia and learning disorders and also, ironically, of high intelligence.

Secret palmist assignment

At last, it's time to throw off your cloak of incognito and show yourself to the world. To gain as much experience as possible, why not offer your services for free at parties, fetes, fairs and exhibitions?

When you give a reading, take your time. Refuse to be rushed. Try to get the person you're reading for to give you feedback. A simple way to proceed that doesn't put you on the spot is to ask questions. Ask the person with short Vitality Lines: 'did your parents create a stable home environment? Do you feel insecure? Do you feel you run out of energy easily?' In this way, you can learn your way around the palm without feeling you have to be all-knowing.

When you've had some experience and practice (at least a year of practice and over a hundred readings, preferably more), you may feel you want to charge people for your services. If you do, always offer a money-back guarantee. This is a wonderful way of expressing confidence in your skills and it provides security and peace of mind for your clients.

If you want to go further and study the art to a more advanced level, purchase and work through all the exercises in my other work: *The Spellbinding Power of Palmistry* (Green Magic, ISBN 0780954723057).

Palmistry is a benign and magical art. Try to use your new-found skills as an opportunity to increase tolerance, peace and understanding.

One last piece of advice. Don't dither. Get going and practice palmistry, right now!

Brain bashing quiz
Time given: ten minutes

1. Give three qualities you might expect to find in the palm of an introvert.
2. Do extroverts naturally hold their fingers close together?
3. Would a deeply repressed person have ten ulnar loops?
4. What are three signs to look for on an open, flexible person's palm?
5. What's the primary indicator of low self-esteem?
6. What other signs might indicate low self-esteem?
7. What's the classic sign of a rebel?
8. If someone had a fragile mental state, would they have a

strong, straight Line of Consciousness?

9. What palm signs might indicate someone with learning difficulties?

Answers are on the next page.

APPENDIX ONE

How to take a palm print

You will need: water-based, block printing ink; an ink roller (both can be obtained from arts and crafts shops) and plain A4 photocopying paper.

Squeeze one centimeter of ink onto a sheet of plastic or any smooth, non-absorbent surface like a glossy magazine cover. Roll the ink (black or a dark color is best) until the roller is covered. Try to use the minimum amount of ink possible. Then roll the ink over the palm with the roller, covering the whole surface including the fingers with an even, thin layer. Everyone tends to tense and stretch out their palm while the ink is applied, but it's best to get your client to relax their hands as much as possible. Follow the contours of the hand and retouch any bare patches.

Place a couple of magazines under the A4 paper and press the

---

1. Introverts have: fingers closed tightly together; silk or coarse skin; faint lines or thick, trench-like ones; a deeply curving Line of Consciousness; tied Lines of consciousness with Vitality Lines and often, long mirror fingers.
2. No. Closed fingers are the sign of an introvert.
3. No. Print pattern wise, ten loops are the sign of an open, expressive person.
4. Ten ulna (normal) loops; composite patterns on thumbs or mirror fingers; flexible fingers; curving major lines, no crossing lines.
5. A short mirror finger is the primary sign of low self-esteem.
6. Radial loops on both mirror fingers; a weak or short Vitality Line; a 'bound' beginning to the Line of Consciousness and the Vitality Line; jealousy lines at the end of the Line of Emotion.
7. A short wall digit is the primary sign of a rebel.
8. No. The Line of Consciousness is likely to be faint, frazzled and broken up if a person's metal state were fragile.
9. A very weak, short, or poorly formed Line of Consciousness; very few, thick, scar like palm lines; a simian line on a very simple palm.

Answers

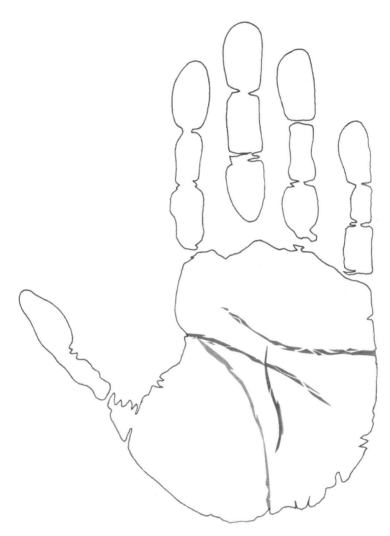

person's palm down onto it with firm pressure, using both of your own hands. Make sure you push down on both the palm *and* the fingers.

Lift the hand off carefully; hold the printed paper down with one hand while you do so. Don't forget to write the qualities that can't be seen onto the print sheet – the skin texture, stiffness of the

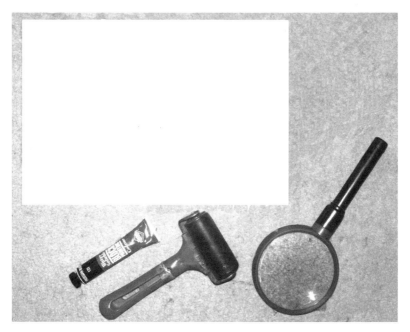

Equipment

fingers and thumb and also the print pattern on the thumb. Then you'll have all the information you need to study the hand properly.

When reading palms, the need for good light can't be over-emphasized. The best, fixed source is a beautician's illuminated magnifying lamp. For mobile use, an illuminated magnifying glass is excellent – it's best to buy a really good quality one from an optometrist. You'll also need a straight-edged ruler to compare finger lengths.

Inking the palm

Press firmly with both your hands

APPENDIX TWO

Hour twelve - reading test answers

Josh's silk skin makes him acutely aware of his surroundings. He picks up moods and atmospheres and is extremely sensitive. He has a delicate physical system that won't tolerate toxins like alcohol. He'd thrive in a calm, gentle environment where his sensitivity could be useful – alternative therapies, or the arts. There is a loop of sensitivity on his palm and this would heighten an already highly-tuned awareness. He may actually be psychic.

Looking at the mirror finger which is short and bent, Josh has real problems reflecting himself and his needs. He's certainly not bossy. He has had an upbringing where his true needs and sense of self were not encouraged to develop. He may seriously neglect himself. He will avoid responsibility and will have issues around a lack of self-worth. The radial loop pattern on this digit exaggerates these traits. He constantly prioritizes others' needs over his own and easily loses his sense of self. The radial loop will add to his high receptivity to others and make him able to 'tune in' to their needs. This sign is common on therapists and care workers. Josh will find criticism extremely difficult to cope with.

Moving onto the thumb. The print here is a composite, giving real problems in motivation. Josh finds it hard to know what course of action to take and can't make his mind up. He meanders from enthusiasm to doubt and back again and often doesn't see a project through. Positively, he's good at seeing others' viewpoints.

The wall finger has a whorl print on it. This gives an original sense of values with a dislike of rules, so he's rebellious (though his sensitivity will make this rebellion somewhat passive). He's sure to have unusual beliefs and probably also an unorthodox lifestyle, and he'd choose freedom over worldly success. There's no loop of industry which might counteract these traits.

The peacock finger is *huge*. Josh has a big persona he hides behind. He has a sense of the dramatic and may take risks in life. He has a strong drive to show off skills on the public eye in some manner. The whorl print gives spatial awareness and an eye for line, form, color and perspective, so there may be skills in this area.

Josh does indeed have a loop of leisure. This strongly prioritizes his need to enjoy life and to not take on a demanding career. It's essential he enjoys his work and he may have made his leisure pursuit his job.

The long antenna digit gives Josh a love of language and communication skills. He may speak another language and loves to communicate. The low-set pattern of this digit indicates father-parent issues. He may have had a distant or absent father figure and he may be a little sexually immature. He may seek older, dominant or simply inappropriate partners until this factor is understood.

Let's check our results by asking Josh to chip in. The following dialogue is a recording in a palmistry class where the students gave a reading from the print while Josh was present.

Josh: 'I'm flabbergasted! This is absolutely amazing. I didn't have any faith at all in palmistry at all, but I do now!

I am very sensitive. I'm a homeopath and clients often say I pick up on what they're going to say before they say it. I can't drink alcohol; it makes me ill. My mother was always too busy with her career to pay much attention to my needs and I learned to get attention by showing off. I still love to show off – I'm in a jazz band and I do a bit of interior decorating. At one time, I was a hairdresser, so the stuff about having a good 'eye' must be right.

I hate responsibility and my partner says it's always her that has to make the decisions, 'cause I never know what to do for the best. I've been dithering about starting a family for five years!

Rebellious, yeah, I'd say I am. I've been a Buddhist for more than ten years and I disagree with everything this government does.

As for the dad thing, I didn't know my father, he left when I was four, so that's about right. As for inappropriate partners, I've certainly had my share of them! And I love to talk and to communicate generally. All in all, I'm hugely impressed and want to do the palmistry course myself. Where do I sign?'

APPENDIX THREE

Quick-reference chart

1. Right hand/Left hand

Active hand - The developed, expressed, outer personality.

Passive hand - The latent, underlying, formative influences and inner personality.

2. Thumb ball

The height and fullness of this mount shows energy reserves.

Full, high and flabby - acute sensuality, but poor muscular development.

Full and firm - passionate, lusty vitality, abundant energy and human warmth.

Full and rock hard - physically strong and hardy, emotively repressive.

Flat - lack of vital energy, general lassitude and emotional coolness.

3. Skin Texture

Silk skin feels: fragile, thin and silky smooth.

giving a receptivity that is: highly sensitive and intuitive, responding to 'vibes' and atmospheres, avoiding conflict.

Paper skin feels: fine and dry, often slightly yellowish, the skin ridges are just perceptible.

giving a receptivity that is: responsive to visual, verbal and information-based stimuli.

Grainy skin feels: slightly rough, with easily-felt skin ridges, the palm is firm, with well-defined lines.

giving a receptivity that is: active, needing stimulus, an avoidance of passive-receptive activities.

Coarse skin feels: hard and rough to the touch – almost abrasive, with few palm lines.

giving a receptivity that is: almost indifferent to pain and temperature, responsive to the physical world and to nature.

4. Finger chart

DIGIT	Mirror	Wall	Peacock	Antenna
Long	a	b	c	d
Short	e	f	n/a	g
FINGERPRINT PATTERN				
Simple arch	h	i	j	k
Whorl	l	m	n	o
Tented arch	p	n/a	n/a	n/a
composite	q	r	n/a	n/a
Radial loop	s	t	n/a	n/a
Low Set	n/a	n/a	n/a	u

a - Self aware, serious, responsible, inclined to perfectionism.

b- Respect for authority or value system, systemized knowledge.

c - Needs a public persona, creative drive, risk taker, flirtatious.

d - Well-developed capacity for communication skills and language.

e - Low self-esteem, lack of early reinforcement.

f - Unconventional, restless, innovative.

g - Not naturally inclined to rich vocabulary and communication skills.

h - Solid, practical, repressive, can lack ambition.

i - Seeks practicality in any philosophy, pragmatic about vocation, the past as basis for values.

j - Inclined to physical forms of self expression, skill in crafts and practical arts.

k - (rare) Pedantic about vocabulary, sexually reticent.

l - Individual, freedom loving, innovative, can be secretive.

m - Quirky lifestyle, original philosophy and values.

n - Originality in arts and fashion sense, keen eye for spatial awareness and perspective.

o - Interests in unusual knowledge, oblique minded, drawn to unusual love matches.

p - (rare) Intense, seeks dramatic gestures and to seek excitement, drawn to lead, teach or motivate, difficult to relax.

q - Perpetually uncertain about who one is, need variety, capacity to see both sides of any situation.

r - Unclear about career choice and philosophy, seeks fairness in life values.

s - Hypersensitive to others' influences, caring, intuitive, insecure.

t - Very open to causes and political groups and alternative values, concerned with obligations to family.

u - Underdevelopment of sexual and intimate articulacy - father issues.

5. Thumb chart

Long	abundant reserves of will and drive, good potential for the development of specialist skills
Short	limited potential for demanding, long-term endeavors
Stiff	self control, self disciplined, application
Bendy	flexible, needs variety, lacks persistence and willpower

Thumb's print pattern

Whorl	can go it alone, unconventional, self-starter
Arch	stubborn, dislikes vague plans, persistent, practical
Composite	variable in approach, indecisive

6. Print patterns on the palm

Loop of leisure priority given to leisure, activities, holidays and hobbies, must find job pleasurable, often avoids serious career.

Loop of industry strong work ethic, industrious, career minded, business-like.

Loop of leadership organizational ability and the inclination to acquire status within a group.

Loop of sensitivity deep inner sensitivity and possible psychic perception, sense of déjà vu, possible artistic sensitivities.

Whorl of isolation self-contained, secretive, odd, artistic. Can feel trapped within or trapped outside of themselves.

Loop of nature open to natural forces, love of nature, an affinity with plants, animals and the countryside.

Composite on Sea of Subconscious ups and downs emotionally, confusion about feelings, inner turmoil.

Arch on Sea of Subconscious emotional reticence and inhibition of spontaneity, affections demonstrated practically.

Loop of inspiration inspires the imagination, artistic mystical, cosmic, religious and often a little weird.

Loop of rhythm sense of rhythm and a love of music.

Loop of courage respect for courage and heroism, a drive to set oneself challenges.

7. Major Lines

LINE	Vitality	Emotion	Lifepath	Consciousness
Strong	a	b	c	d
Weak	e	f	g	h
Curved	i	j	k	l
Straight	m	n	o	p
Broken	q	r	s	t

a - Deep rooted sense of security, grounded, adequate vitality, ability to sustain cyclic patterns, self-supporting, stable.

b - Good awareness of emotional processes, receptive, open, resonant, responsive, empathic

c - Strong sense of personal choice and direction, own values, resistance to outside influences, self knowing, strong character.

d - Good conceptual and cognitive framework, sense of personal vision, switched on, effective, coherent conceptually.

e - Poor patterns of sleep, ungrounded, insecure, no sense of permanence, easily uprooted, needs support, lacks energy.

f - Weak emotional connections, unaware, lacks resonance, poor receptivity and empathy

g - Poorly defined as a person, follows other's ideals of success, poor self knowledge, uncertain life choices, lacks balance, no personal goals.

h - Incoherent mentally, poor concentration, ineffective, shy and timid, no thoughts and opinions of one's own, lacks mental clarity.

i - It's normal and average for this line to be curved.

j - Curved (upwards) romantic, expressive, emotional processes directed to some sort of ideal. (downwards), expresses opposite sex qualities.

k - Curved (from Sea of Subconscious) social connections and relationships very important, own needs prioritized, artistic leanings, work involves personal and social skills, different values to parents.

l - Subjective, personal worldview, inclined to be colorful and intuitive in perceptions, interested in processes more than facts.

m - The Vitality Line is never straight.

n - No emotional ideals, not romantic, impatient, hot blooded.

o - Well balanced, even personality, a straightforward person, uncomplicated in ambitions, clear priorities and goals in life.

p - Level headed, direct, logical, objective and factual, mental projections of the real world. Black and white view.

q - Major seismic shift in lifestyle, involving disruptions to home, family or health.

r - Interruption in emotional life, likely to divorce, or experience loss or trauma, eventual new love leading to a new emotional plane.

s - Break in life path, usually temporary loss of work, direction and goals.

t - Crisis of understanding, possible mental breakdown leading to a complete change of personality and world view.

8. Minor Lines

Fantasy line

Description: above and parallel to the Line of Emotion.

Interpretation: vivid imagination, drive to escape the mundane through arts, entertainment, spirituality or drugs.

A fragmented form of the line inclines the person to be highly strung, sensitive and introverted.

Affection lines

Description: lines on the extreme outer edge of the palm, beneath the antenna finger. Only if extending onto the face of the palm are they relevant.

Interpretation: long straight line – a search for the 'right' partner will dominate the persons love life; plunging towards the Line of Emotion or crossing it - a subliminal inclination to difficult relationships and a high incidence of divorce or serious losses in love; cuts upward around the antenna finger - remains outside of the mating game for long periods; may have celibate relationships.

Passion line

Description: straight slanted line running from the mid-section of the Line of Emotion to the base of the antenna finger.

Interpretation: an indication of a highly visual, voyeuristic and imaginary aspect to a person's sexuality.

Inner Realm line

Description: vertical, straight, fine, line beneath the peacock finger.

Interpretation: (only if the line is present beneath the Line of Emotion is it notable) a sense of oneness with a process, a need for peace and quiet, internal contentment, the need to be alone, an inner life.

Nervous Activity line

Description: fine vertical line or series of small lines mid-palm, beneath the antenna finger.

Interpretation: if fine and clear, it bestows the capacity for mental concentration and inspiration; if striated, islanded or trough-like, it indicates an agitated nervousness and digestive and nervous complaints.

Spirit Line

Description: A fine, long, clear, curved line in the same location as the Nervous Activity line.

Interpretation: it gives the capacity for psychic perception.

Battle Line

Description: within the Vitality Line, close to the thumb, only if clear and unbroken and longer than two centimeters is it relevant.

Interpretation: physical drive, a battling nature, the need for challenges, prevalent amongst athletes and sports people.

Loyalty line

Description: broad, horizontal line, crossing from thumb to Vitality

Line.

Interpretation: an instinctive, tribal loyalty, which may be to the local football team, partner, family or place.

Intensity line

Description: a fine, horizontal, straight, line in the Sea of Subconscious.

Interpretation: stress in the emotional field, the need to be stimulated and stirred up; a thrill seeker.

Allergy Line

Description: a curved line in the Sea of Subconscious.

Interpretation: an over-responsive immune system and generally, the presence of allergies.

Fingertip bars

Description: small horizontal lines on the fingertips.

Interpretation: stress/disturbance to the endocrinal system.

Samaritan lines

Description: fine, horizontal lines crossing the Line of Emotion under the antenna digit.

Interpretation: associated with carers of all kinds - complimentary therapists, nurses, healers, and simple 'good neighbors'.

Ring of Solomon

Description: a fine line around the base of the mirror finger.

Interpretation: gives insight into the nature of others, a natural inclination to analyze.

Teacher's square
Location: a fine square formed from lines under the mirror finger.

Interpretation: gives qualities of people management.

Aspiration lines
Location: fine short lines rising up from the Vitality Line towards the mirror finger.

Interpretation: a new job, new child, a better situation, positive attitudes and achievements.

Stress lines
Location: fine lines running across the Primal Home and Body quadrant.

Interpretation: stress within the home environment.

APPENDIX FOUR

BIBLIOGRAPHY

Websites

The web is awash with palmistry sites, unfortunately many are a mixture of psychobabble and superstition. A couple of good sites to get you started are:

www.handresearch.com

www.handanalysis.co.uk

My own website at **www. johnnyfincham.com** will provide you with an up-to-date list.

Bibliography

Brandon-Jones D. 'Your palm, barometer of health' (1985 Rider) Brown, W M & Finn, B. Cooke & S.M. Breedlove A preliminary investigation of the associations between personality ,cognitive ability and digit ratio in personality and Individual Differences, (Archives of sexual behavior, vol.31, no.1, feb, p.123-177)

Cummins and Midlo 'Dermatagyphic analysis as diagnostic tool' (Medicine 46, 35 USA) 'Finger prints palms and soles', (1943 New York, Dover publications)'

David T. J. 'The palmer axial triradius, a new method of location' (Human Heredity. 21, 624)

Denton B. 'Principal component analysis of the elongaton of the metacarpal and phalangeal bones' (Am. Jour. Phys Anthropol. Sept 1977)

Digby Roll 1V Ms 13th Cent. (Bodleian library, Oxford)

Greenough, Black and Wallace Experience and brain
development. *Child Development, 58*, 539-559. 1987

Gutiérrez B *Dermatoglyphic abnormalities in psychosis: a twin
study* (Society of Biological Psychiatry, vol.41, p.624-626)

Hummel F. 'Ipsilateral cortical activation of increasing
complexity representation' (Clinical Neurophysiology April
2003)

Hutchinson B. 'Your life in your hands' 1967 (Sphere)

Jaquin N. 'The hand speaks' 1942 London

Johnson CF, Opitz E. 'Unusual palm creases and unusual
children. The Sydney line and "type C" palmar lines and their
clinical significance in a child development clinic' (Clin Pediatr
(Phila). 1973 Feb;12(2):101-12).

Jones C. 'The interpretation of dermatoglyphic patterns' (1992
Swan Paradise)

Kimura D & P.G. Clarke ~ *Congenital dermatoglyphic
malformations in severe bipolar disorder* (Psychiatry Research,
78, p.133-140)

Manning J. 'Digit Ratio: A Pointer to Fertility, Behavior and
Health' (2002 NJ: Rutgers University Press).; 'Long ring digit,
pointer to autism?' (New Scientist March 2001), 'Depression
index' (9/00 Am. Journ. of Evolution and Behaviour) 'Sex role
identity related to ratio of 2nd and 4th digit in women.'
(Biological Psychology Feb 2003); '2nd to 4th digit ratio
(2D:4D) and number of sex partners: evidence for effects of
prenatal testosterone in men' (Psychoneuroendocrinology.
(2006 Jan;31(1):30-7); 'The ratio of 2nd to 4th digit length and
performance in skiing'. (Jour. Sports Med. Phys. Fitness Dec
2002); '2nd to 4th digit ration and offspring sex ratio' (Jour.

Theor. Biol. July 2002) 'The ratio of 2nd to 4th digit length – a proxy for testosterone and susceptibility to AIDS?' (Med. Hypotheses Dec 2001)

Napier J. Hands (1980 Allen and Unwin)

Penrose 'Recent advances in human genetics' (LS1965 Churchill).

Raham Q. 'Sexual orientation and the 2nd to 4th finger length ratio: evidence for organising effects of sex hormones or developmental instability?'

Roonney, JR and Maestripieri D, Relative finger lengths predict men's behavior and attractiveness during social interactions with women -(Endocrinology April 2003)

Wolffe C. 'The hand in psychological diagnosis' (Methuen London)

O

is a symbol of the world,
of oneness and unity. O Books
explores the many paths of wholeness
and spiritual understanding which
different traditions have developed down
the ages. It aims to bring this knowledge
in accessible form, to a general readership,
providing practical spirituality to today's seekers.

For the full list of over 200 titles covering:

- CHILDREN'S PRAYER, NOVELTY AND GIFT BOOKS
- CHILDREN'S CHRISTIAN AND SPIRITUALITY
- CHRISTMAS AND EASTER
- RELIGION/PHILOSOPHY
- SCHOOL TITLES
- ANGELS/CHANNELLING
- HEALING/MEDITATION
- SELF-HELP/RELATIONSHIPS
- ASTROLOGY/NUMEROLOGY
- SPIRITUAL ENQUIRY
- CHRISTIANITY, EVANGELICAL
AND LIBERAL/RADICAL
- CURRENT AFFAIRS
- HISTORY/BIOGRAPHY
- INSPIRATIONAL/DEVOTIONAL
- WORLD RELIGIONS/INTERFAITH
- BIOGRAPHY AND FICTION
- BIBLE AND REFERENCE
- SCIENCE/PSYCHOLOGY

Please visit our website,
www.O-books.net

SOME RECENT O BOOKS

The 7 Ahas! of Highly Enlightened Souls
How to free yourself from ALL forms of stress
Mike George
7th printing
A very profound, self empowering book. Each page bursting with wisdom and insight. One you will need to read and reread over and over again! **Paradigm Shift**
1903816319 128pp 190/135mm **£5.99 $11.95**

God Calling
A Devotional Diary
A. J. Russell
46th printing
Perhaps the best-selling devotional book of all time, over 6 million copies sold.
1905047428 280pp 135/95mm **£7.99** cl.
US rights sold

The Goddess, the Grail and the Lodge
The Da Vinci code and the real origins of religion
Alan Butler
5th printing
This book rings through with the integrity of sharing time-honoured revelations. As a historical detective, following a golden thread from the great Megalithic cultures, Alan Butler vividly presents a

compelling picture of the fight for life of a great secret and one that we simply can't afford to ignore. From the foreword by **Lynn Picknett** & **Clive Prince**

1903816696 360pp 230/152mm **£12.99 $19.95**

The Heart of Tantric Sex

A sourcebook on the practice of Tantric sex

Diana Richardson

3rd printing

One of the most revolutionary books on sexuality ever written. Ruth Ostrow, News Ltd.

1903816378 256pp **£9.99 $14.95**

I Am With You

The best-selling modern inspirational classic

John Woolley

14th printing hardback

Probably the consistently best-selling devotional in the UK today.

0853053413 280pp 150x100mm **£9.99** cl

4th printing paperback

1903816998 280pp 150/100mm **£6.99 $12.95**

In the Light of Meditation

The art and practice of meditation in 10 lessons

Mike George

2nd printing

A classy book. A gentle yet satisfying pace and is beautifully illustrated. Complete with a CD or guided meditation commentaries, this is a true gem among meditation guides. **Brainwave**

1903816610 224pp 235/165mm full colour throughout +CD **£11.99 $19.95**

The Instant Astrologer
A revolutionary new book and software package for the astrological seeker
Lyn Birkbeck
2nd printing
The brilliant Lyn Birkbeck's new book and CD package, The Instant Astrologer, *combines modern technology and the wisdom of the ancients, creating an invitation to enlightenment for the masses, just when we need it most!*
Astrologer **Jenny Lynch**, Host of NYC's StarPower Astrology Television Show
1903816491 628pp full colour throughout with CD ROM 240/180 **£39 $69** cl

Is There An Afterlife?
A comprehensive overview of the evidence, from east and west
David Fontana
2nd printing
An extensive, authoritative and detailed survey of the best of the evidence supporting survival after death. It will surely become a classic not only of parapsychology literature in general but also of survival literature in particular. Professor Fontana is to be congratulated on this landmark study and I thoroughly recommend it to all who are really interested in a serious exploration of the subject. **Universalist**
1903816904 496pp 230/153mm **£14.99 $24.95**

The Reiki Sourcebook

Bronwen and Frans Stiene

5th printing

It captures everything a Reiki practitioner will ever need to know about the ancient art. This book is hailed by most Reiki professionals as the best guide to Reiki. For an average reader, it's also highly enjoyable and a good way to learn to understand Buddhism, therapy and healing. **Michelle Bakar**, *Beauty magazine*

1903816556 384pp **£12.99 $19.95**

Soul Power

The transformation that happens when you know

Nikki de Carteret

4th printing

This may be one of the finest books in its genre today. Using scenes from her own life and growth, Nikki de Carteret weaves wisdom about soul growth and the power of love and transcendent wisdom gleaned from the writings of the mystics. This is a book that I will read gain and again as a reference for my own soul growth. She is a scholar who is totally accessible and grounded in the human experience. **Barnes and Noble review**

190381636X 240pp **£9.99 $15.95**

Back to the Truth

5,000 years of Advaita

Dennis Waite

A wonderful book. Encyclopedic in nature, and destined to become a classic. **James Braha**, author of *Living Reality*

Absolutely brilliant...an ease of writing with a water-tight argument outlining the great universal truths. This book will become a modern classic. A milestone in the history of Advaita. **Paula Marvelly**, author of *The Teachers of One*

1905047614 500pp **£19.95 $29.95**

Beyond Photography
Encounters with orbs, angels and mysterious light forms
Katie Hall and John Pickering

The authors invite you to join them on a fascinating quest; a voyage of discovery into the nature of a phenomenon, manifestations of which are shown as being historical and global as well as contemporary and intently personal.

At journey's end you may find yourself a believer, a doubter or simply an intrigued wonderer... Whatever the outcome, the process of journeying is likely prove provocative and stimulating and - as with the mysterious images fleetingly captured by the authors' cameras - inspiring and potentially enlightening. **Brian Sibley**, author and broadcaster.

1905047908 272pp 50 b/w photos +8pp colour insert **£12.99 $24.95**

Don't Get MAD Get Wise
Why no one ever makes you angry, ever!
Mike George

There is a journey we all need to make, from anger, to peace, to forgiveness. Anger always destroys, peace always restores, and forgiveness always heals. This little book explains the journey, the steps you can take to make it happen for you.

1905047827 160pp **£7.99 $14.95**

IF You Fall...

I always thought I'ld rather be dead than paralysed: One slip, one moment, and everything changes...

Karen Darke

Karen Darke's story is about the indomitability of spirit, from one of life's cruel vagaries of fortune to what is insight and inspiration. She has overcome the limitations of paralysis and discovered a life of challenge and adventure that many of us only dream about. It is all about the mind, the spirit and the desire that some of us find, but which all of us possess. **Joe Simpson**, mountaineer and author of *Touching the Void*

1905047886 240pp **£9.99 $19.95**

Love, Healing and Happiness

Spiritual wisdom for a post-secular era

Larry Culliford

Larry Culliford has a remarkable gift for making connections between psychology and spirituality, and for linking our basic human needs with divine love. This is a wonderful book for those who are searching for 'life in all its fullness'. It draws on secular and religious wisdom to speak to men and women who are looking for a spirituality that meets them where they are. **Rt Rev Dominic Walker**, Bishop of Monmouth.

1905047916 224pp **£10.99 $19.95**

The Marriage of Jesus

The lost wife of the hidden years

Maggy Whitehouse

The "missing years" in the Bible are those he spent as a husband,

raising his family. Given that the average life-span of a woman 2000 years ago was 27 years and two out of three women died in childbirth, Jesus was probably a widower when he began teaching. So what happened to Jesus' wife, this most forgotten of women?
1846940087 260pp **£11.99 $19.95**

Punk Science
Inside the mind of God
Manjir Samanta-Laughton

Wow! Punk Science is an extraordinary journey from the microcosm of the atom to the macrocosm of the Universe and all stops in between. Manjir Samanta-Laughton's synthesis of cosmology and consciousness is sheer genius. It is elegant, simple and, as an added bonus, makes great reading. **Dr Bruce H. Lipton**, author of *The Biology of Belief*
1905047932 320pp **£12.95 $22.95**

Rosslyn Revealed
A secret library in stone
Alan Butler

Rosslyn Revealed gets to the bottom of the mystery of the chapel featured in the Da Vinci Code. The results of a lifetime of careful research and study demonstrate that truth really is stranger than fiction; a library of philosophical ideas and mystery rites, that were heresy in their time, have been disguised in the extraordinarily elaborate stone carvings.
1905047924 260pp b/w + colour illustrations **£19.95 $29.95** cl

The Way of Thomas
Nine Insights for Enlightened Living from the Secret Sayings of Jesus
John R. Mabry

What is the real story of early Christianity? Can we find a Jesus that is relevant as a spiritual guide for people today?

These and many other questions are addressed in this popular presentation of the teachings of this mystical Christian text. Telling the story of this gospels loss and recent recovery, readers will learn how Jesus' original community was eclipsed by followers of Paul, and how Jesus' true teaching was subverted and buried under centuries of fabricated history.

1846940303 196pp **£10.99 $19.95**

The Way Things Are
A Living Approach to Buddhism
Lama Ole Nydahl

An up-to-date and revised edition (three times the length) of a seminal work in the Diamond Way Buddhist tradition, that makes the timeless wisdom of Buddhism accessible to western audiences. Lama Ole has established more than 450 centres in 43 countries.

1846940427 240pp **£9.99 $19.95**